THE PSYCHO-ETHICAL ASPECTS OF ABHIDHAMMA

Rina Sircar

University Press of America,® Inc.
Lanham • New York • Oxford

4720 Boston Way
Lanham, Maryland 20706

12 Hid's Copse Rd.
Cumnor Hill, Oxford OX2 9JJ

Printed in the United States of America
British Library Cataloging in Publication Information Available

Library of Congress Cataloging-in-Publication Data

Sircar, Rina
The psycho-ethical aspects of Abhidhamma / Rina Sircar.
p. cm.
Includes bibliographical references.
1. Abhidharma. 2. Buddhism—Psychology. 3. Buddhist ethics.
4. Conduct of life. 5. Religious life—Buddhism.
BQ4195.S54 1999 294.3'422—dc21 98-32321 CIP

ISBN 0-7618-1322-5 (cloth: alk. ppr.)
ISBN 0-7618-1323-3 (pbk: alk. ppr.)

™ The paper used in this publication meets the minimum requirements of American National Standard for Information Sciences—Permanence of Paper for Printed Library Materials, ANSI Z39.48—1984

This book is dedicated to

Dr. Haridas Chaudhuri, the founder of the California Institute of Integral Studies, who invited me to come and teach in San Francisco. His boundless support and guidance was priceless;

Very Venerable Taungpulu Sayadaw, my saintly teacher whose presence and light were deeply felt while writing this book;

Dr. K.P. Sircar, my most beloved brother and brother to all. This book would not have seen the light of day without his constant support and encouragement. This book is as much his as mine.

Contents

Foreword

Practical Buddhism is said to consist of three higher educations *(adhiśikśā):* those of ethics *(sīla),* mind or meditation *(citta, samādhi),* and wisdom *(prajñā).* All three of these are essential for the attainment of freedom from suffering which is perfect enlightenment; no one of them alone will suffice. Yet if any one of them is most essential, is the actual sword that cuts the knots of entanglement in the unenlightened life of suffering, it is wisdom. This is the wisdom of selflessness, the perfect insight into the true nature of self and reality that constitutes a buddha's enlightenment. Doctrinal Buddhism is arranged to correspond exactly to the practical. Of the Three Baskets of Buddhist teachings, the Discipline (*Vinaya*) teaches ethics, the Discourses (*Sutra*) teach meditation, and the Clear Science (Higher Teachings), the *Abhidharma*, teaches wisdom. Therefore, to actually attain enlightenment, some form of *Abhidharma* teaching is indispensable.

Abhidharma has the fearsome reputation of being somewhat dry and difficult, perhaps originally deriving from the fact that in traditional Buddhist societies only monks and nuns learned it, lay people contenting themselves with *Sutras* and some of the exemplary narratives that constitute the *Vinaya*. The *Vinaya* is about the Buddha and the monastic community; it is the history of their lives and their growth as a community, incorporating the ethical judgments he delivered in individual cases. The *Sutras* are discourses delivered by the Buddha to specific audiences in specific times and places. The *Abhidharma* is only authorized by the enlightened masters he trained. It presents the inner structure of the process of teaching and learning in the form of schemas or matrices (*mātrikā*) which are memorized by the practitioner then used as a framework for profound meditative practices. Therefore, when you really want to put the Buddhist teaching into practice, when you decide it is really necessary to realize its meaning, you must study the *Abhidharma*.

In this context, it is a relief and a joy to encounter the *Abhidharma* explained so clearly, calmly, exactly, and expressively by Rina Sircar in this excellent book. She opens up for us the most important elements of the fundamental structure of the *Dharma*, helps us understand them and makes them usable for our critical meditations.

She also brings to the subject a distinctively passionate voice, a profound care and respect for the vast and unfathomable wisdom of the Buddha and the great masters that succeeded him down through the centuries, up to her own beloved Taungpulu Sayadaw, and even to herself. It is an honor and a pleasure to introduce and recommend to general attention this extraordinary gem of a guidebook which will take the reader to the deepest, richest waters in the great ocean of Buddhist teachings.

Robert A. F. Thurman
New York, NY
August 4, 1998

Preface

I feel very fortunate to have been born in Burma—now Myanmar—as Burma is the land of the Golden Pagodas where one can enshrine Dhamma in the heart and can be encouraged at every turn to spread good will and loving kindness all around. I was born in Pyapon District, a small township in the delta region where rice fields dominate the landscape. I fondly recall the closeness of the people and the fun we had in our small village.

Growing up in a Buddhist country close to a monastic atmosphere, I imbibed its ennobling qualities. After graduating from Pyapon State High School, I had to leave my peaceful country life for Rangoon where I joined the University. It was in Rangoon that I met the Very Venerable Taungpulu Sayadaw, the saint from the forest, who left his hut in the arid plains of Burma to visit our family at the invitation of my brother. He became our spiritual guide and with his blessings I began in earnest to study Abhidhamma and Pāli language, and so stepped onto the centuries-old path tread by so many scholars and saints before me.

I was blessed to meet Aggamahapandita Venerable U Thittila as well, a giant in knowledge about the Tipiṭaka and Pāli language who had taught in Oxford University for several years and translated *The Book of Analysis* (*Vibhaṅga*) along with Mrs. Rhys Davids and I.B. Horner of the London Pali Text Society. He rarely spoke about himself and his vast achievements, so focused was he on the subject for which he was famous. When I took several of my students to meet him in 1977, his greeting to me was, "What is the difference between intuition and insight?" For my studies of *Paṭṭhāna,* the longest book in the *Abhidhamma Piṭaka,* I was fortunate to sit at the feet of another giant, the Venerable U Narada, known as Paṭṭhāna Sayadaw, and Venerable Thazi Sayadaw, a close associate of the Very Venerable Taungpulu Kaba-Aye Sayadaw. Their humility, patience, and kindness were added qualities to their vast knowledge, and they passed on to countless students the abstruse formulas clarified by the stories and explanations which are part and parcel of a still living oral tradition.

Through the years I have tried my best to write clearly and simply for my Western students. There are many topics in Abhidhamma worthy of exploration which would be of great benefit for our troubled times. Abhidhamma, which is primarily a psychology, goes beyond the intellectual and emotional boundaries drawn by Western psychology and demands validation of its claims through the direct experience of meditation. It is not just to be studied, but to be applied to our daily lives. This book fulfills a long-standing desire to offer Abhidhamma to the English speaking world. I am convinced that if suitably presented, Abhidhamma can engage and enrich non-Buddhist thought in the fields of philosophy and applied psychology.

Acknowledgments

It is a happy custom that writers of books have an opportunity to extend their gratitude to those who have made a notable contribution in one way or another to their production. In my case, this book contains the voices and hearts of many, so thanks are due in all directions. Without the heartfelt encouragement of these friends, no doubt, I would still be writing the introduction.

I must first acknowledge and express my gratitude to my venerable teachers, students, and family members who have influenced me and collaborated with me through the years of study and teaching. Because of them, this book has been a labor of love. To one individual I owe more than words can say, John Paul Lenny, for whom this book was tied into a publishing schedule. I am especially thankful to Linda Carson who, as my student and well-wisher, was one of the first to encourage me in to publish this work. Also, for my close association with Dr. Harry Prochaska, a Jungian analyst; Warren Sokolis, psychotherapist; Marcus Keil, founding member of our forest monastery in Boulder Creek, California, and Kim Criswell, my meditation student and friend, I am deeply indebted. All of them patiently read the manuscript and offered invaluable suggestions for its improvement.

I am forever indebted to Dr. Kartikeya Patel, all-around genius and East-West scholar, and to Dr. Anne Teich, student of Abhidhamma, who continued the editing process and oversaw the book to completion. To Dr. Varasambodhi Bhikkhu, my profoundest respect and gratitude; he was a source of many valuable improvements. And for their generous donation of technical support, I am ever grateful to Richard Teich and Francia Friendlich.

Finally, there is really no adequate way I can extend my gratitude to Dr. Robert A.F. Thurman who, as one of the most active Buddhist scholars and Bodhisattvas alive today, and with hardly any time to put his feet on the ground, agreed out of his compassion to write the Foreword. I honor and respect his sacrifice.

Namo Tassa Bhagavato Arahato Sammāsambuddho

Introduction

As a teacher of Abhidhamma in the West for the past 25 years I am frequently asked to modernize the language of the Abhidhamma, the ancient psychological teachings of the Buddha. The entire teaching of Abhidhamma is the result of Buddha's own insights into human nature. It was developed from Buddha's earliest teachings and has been preserved very carefully by the Theravada school so that its authenticity will not be lost.

As a prototype of Eastern psychology, Abhidhamma presents us with a set of concepts for understanding mental health, but it differs noticeably from Western psychotherapy. Abhidhamma points out how one can perfect one's self through understanding the workings of the mind. Mind is such a subtle and intricate phenomenon that it is not possible to find two human beings of the same mind. Thoughts are translated into speech and action which give rise to habits, which in turn form character. Character is the result of a person's mind-directed activities and thus the character of human beings varies. The great pioneer of the psyche, Carl Jung, speaks of two types of character: the introvert and the extrovert who relate their experiences through four functions: thinking, feeling, intuition, and sensation. By contrast the *Visuddhi Magga* (*Path of Purification*) mentions six main types of character or temperament:[1]

Greedy/lustful type (*rāga carita*) - characterized by wanting and craving
Angry/hateful type (*dosa carita*) - characterized by anger and disliking
Deluded type (*moha carita*) - characterized by mental dullness
Faithful type (*saddhā carita*) - characterized by faith, trust, and confidence
Intelligent type (*buddhi carita*) - characterized by intelligence
Speculative type (*vitakka carita*) - characterized by obsessive speculation and "wondering" about this or that

During the Buddha's time there were many wealthy followers who surrendered their pride and possessions at the feet of the Buddha because such things brought them no lasting happiness. Among the followers were beautiful women who at first had refused to meet the Buddha, looking upon his doctrine with disdain. Sometimes he used his supernormal powers to convince them that beauty is only skin deep, and that ultimately, there will be decay, old age, and death.

Why should we allow ourselves to suffer so much? After all, we are born as human beings, the highest of all creations. In one of his discourses the Buddha said, "Born as a human being, why float aimlessly in the ocean of ignorance?" Start cultivating the mind so that the sublime states of consciousness which are latent in the human heart can grow. I think now, more than ever, is the time to practice on a global scale the development of higher grades of consciousness. Once the consciousness is cultivated, the mind will be filled with love, compassion, sympathetic joy, and equanimity. Then we can fight the degrading forces of greed, hatred, pride, etc. which cause dangerous divisions. Once these unwholesome consciousnesses are released from the hearts of humanity, all divisions—creed, color, religion and gender—will melt away. Then only one creed will be clear and distinct and that is the creed of humanity. So let us cultivate the higher grades of consciousness, for it is the way out of all entanglements.

Once a few disciples of the Buddha asked him how to solve the entanglements of life. The Buddha smiled and said, "Go and clean your mind." The disciples said, "Venerable Sir, is that all? It will be not so difficult. Just the mind and nothing else?" The Buddha said, "Yes." "Then give us the instruction now, Lord." The Buddha started talking about the mind and its power, which is beyond that of any machine that has ever been invented. As the Buddha introduced the Abhidhamma, the disciples realized it was not so easy to clean the mind. To start with we must know the mind—what it is and how it works—and for that we must go to the Abhidhamma, the Third Basket of Buddha's teachings. Just as in the Buddha's time, we are all entangled in a tangle—the inner tangle and the outer tangle. The question put forward to the Buddha was, "Who succeeds in disentangling the tangle?" He answered, "He who succeeds in disentangling this tangle is the wise man, established in proper discipline, who has developed consciousness and understanding."[2]

In the storehouse of humankind, which is the mind, there are wholesome as well as unwholesome states of consciousness. How they are organized depends on our point of view, but the Buddha maintained that every unwholesome consciousness has its opposite wholesome consciousness.

One very powerful destructive unwholesome state of mind is anger (*dosa*). The sweet wholesome force which subdues this evil force in the heart is lovingkindness (*metta*). The late Dr. Haridas Chaudhuri, philosopher, teacher, and yogi, called this force, the "alchemy of love,"[3] because of its transforming power on others as well as oneself. "If we are capable of loving others in this unconditional way, we change them and kindle the spirit of love within them. Nothing can be a greater gift than this."[4]

Cruelty (*vihiṁsā*) is another evil force that is responsible for the epidemics of violence which persist in the world. Compassion (*karuṇā*) is its antidote. There is a wonderful story of how a man practiced compassion. His name was Shantidev, and he sat in meditation day and night trying to develop compassion towards all beings. One day, a very high deity decided to test his intentions. He appeared to Shantidev in the form of a suffering dog who was covered with ulcerous sores. The sight of the dog in such a piteous condition moved Shantidev deeply and he immediately went over to see how he could help. "I will wash this poor creature and clean his wounds," he thought. But as he got ready to wash, he realized that there were tiny creatures crawling all over the ulcers and he stopped, thinking, "If I wash the dog's body, then all these creatures will die!" Not wishing to harm any life, he resolved, "I will put out my tongue and slowly take away the creatures from the dog's body." Shantidev closed his eyes, slowly put out his tongue, and moved toward the dog, ready to carry out his plan. At that moment the dog transformed back into the deity who appeared before Shantidev in his true, splendorous form. He told Shantidev that he was testing him to see if his vow to practice compassion was real or just a whim.

Jealousy (*issā*) is another very strong force that poisons one's system and leads to unhealthy rivalries and dangerous competition. Jealous people cannot feel happy when others are progressing. They only rejoice over the failures and misfortunes of others. The most effective remedy for this poison is sympathetic joy (*mudita*) or appreciative joy. Just like the mother who feels happiness at her own child's happiness, so we should practice these feelings even towards strangers.

We human beings always react to pleasurable and non-pleasurable situations with restless excitement or irksome worry (*uddhacca-kukkucca*). The result is that we lose mental balance or evenness of mind. These subtle forces can be eliminated by developing equanimity (*upekkhā*). Once a man who owned a handsome horse woke up to find that it had disappeared. His wife and neighbors thought it odd that upon discovering his loss, he reacted with neither anger nor despair. One day, the horse reappeared with another horse! Once again, the man's friends and neighbors noticed that he was not over-excited nor joyful at this fortunate occurrence.

These are examples of how we can elevate our mind and our consciousness to higher levels which in Buddhism are called the Four Sublime States (*brahma-vihāra*): lovingkindness, compassion, sympathetic joy, and equanimity. Cultivating these four is the first step towards mastering the mind. This process is the true road to power where the ordinary being becomes a supernormal being. These four sublime states of consciousness are also called "illimitables." They are so called because they find no barrier nor limit and can be radiated to the entire universe. They should be extended towards all beings without exception, both to human and animal. To develop these sublime states of consciousness, we have to purify our thoughts, words, and deeds; only then will the sublime states arise and be effective. When we really develop these sublime states of consciousness, our hearts will become free from greed, fear, frustration, anxiety, jealousy, and cruelty.

Among the favorite teachings for purification of the late Very Venerable Taungpulu Sayadaw, a forest dwelling monk and meditation master of Upper Burma, is the very profound and powerful *32 Parts of the Body* meditation. In this instruction, the meditator reflects methodically on the inner and outer body encased by the skin and full of different parts from the soles up and from the hair of the head down thinking thus: "There are in this body, hair of the head, hair of the body, nails, teeth, flesh, sinews, bones, etc." Thus he lives contemplating impermanence, insubstantiality, and impurity in this body. This practice is one of several practices for establishing mindfulness of the body (*kāyagatasatipaṭṭhāna*) and is mentioned in the Great Discourse on the Establishment of Mindfulness (*Satipaṭṭhāna Sutta*) given by the Buddha.

Although exceedingly powerful, this particular practice may not be a suitable and agreeable meditation for everyone, whether a Westerner or an Easterner. No one likes to regard the body as unattractive or foul. However, if we focus our mind deep inside the body such a practice slowly but surely reveals to us the real nature of this body: subject to birth, disease, decay, old age, and death. No magic, miracle, or even scientific power can ever transform these intrinsic mechanisms, and so, it is a characteristic result of this practice that one abandons both pessimism and optimism with regards to the body. The powerful insights gained from the *32 Parts of the Body* meditation make it especially suitable for the person of lustful temperament (*rāgacarita*), but the Venerable Taungpulu Sayadaw recommended it to everyone because it is the surest, and quickest practice for producing both tranquillity and detachment. When we have purified our mind, we will be able to see into the past as well as ahead into the future; we will be able to see into other people's minds; we will have celestial ears, eyes, noses, etc. Also, we will be able to see beings in all the different planes of existence. But this is not all, and it is not the end. To come up to this point, that is, to the higher grades of consciousness, one needs to develop one's mind through the study of Abhidhamma; it is an essential activity for it enriches, purifies, and expands the mind and aids in the progress of meditation.

In Abhidhamma mind is regarded as a sixth sense faculty, and it is treated as inseparable from the body, thus, mentality-materiality becomes the main topic of consideration which is why Abhidhamma is said to be a profound and subtle subject, as well as abstract and dry. This book attempts first and foremost to make the topic interesting so that readers will be encouraged to study this subject in-depth and find out for themselves how even a cursory understanding of the subject can be invaluable in daily life. After his enlightenment, the Buddha organized the knowledge he had acquired through meditation. After the Buddha's passing, this body of knowledge came to be called Abhidhamma.

By studying the Abhidhamma, one will definitely learn how to become whole and integrated, with a harmonious personality and sense of spiritual well-being. This unique traditional Buddhist psychology will help one see the beauty of all things within the awareness of change; with practice, if one is fortunate enough, the result will be the attainment of supreme wisdom. In one of the seven books of Abhidhamma, *The Designation of Human Types* (*Puggala-Paññati*), there is a great deal of exploration of different personality types and temperaments. The book discusses how the unwholesome temperament can be subdued by contemplation on suitable objects of meditation from the Abhidhamma or Buddhist depth psychological point of view.

Buddhist psychology is so deep and profound that if properly studied, our understanding of the mind will become penetratingly clear. For example, to understand the full meaning of "good action," one must start with the first book of the Abhidhamma and follow the theme all the way through the seventh book which is the last. The exposition of that particular "good action" runs all through the seven books of the Abhidhamma Piṭaka in order to fully illuminate its meaning. I feel from my own experience that the study of Abhidhamma can make our lives light like a passing cloud and firm like the highest summit.

Modern humanity is entangled in all sorts of contradictory ideas, views, opinions, and ideologies, both wise and stupid, and our thinking can easily become confused and obsessive. The therapeutic relationship is set up to help individuals in the process of becoming whole and to strengthen their sense of self. Sooner or later the question arises, "Who am I?" and for the student of Abhidhamma, "How can there be no self?" After all, the great prescription of Socrates was, "Know thyself." The intrigue and fear surrounding the concept of identity is never-ending, especially for the Western person whose culture not only promotes individual identity but rewards it. However, the partial understanding of identity prevalent in the West can lead to an "identity crisis" and all too often to the therapist's office. This identity question is dealt with in Abhidhamma from the first book to the last book in a very meaningful yet abstract way.

One of the goals of this book is to avoid the traditional cataloging process which invites tedium and update the old fashioned language of Abhidhamma by using modern language, but without losing the essence or authenticity of the teachings. By modern language I mean supplementing the rich ethical flavor of the classical psychology of Buddhism. We must ever seek new sources to develop a healthy, wholesome, productive sense of moral character devoid of pathological guilt and worry; both are strong hindrances to spiritual growth. Having studied with a meditation master, I have concluded that the true understanding of Abhidhamma does not lie in the head but in the heart itself. Thus, the study of Abhidhamma can have therapeutic results as the Abhidhamma reveals pathways out of pain, conflict, confusion and the miseries of life.

During a time of crisis or when misfortune falls, one's fortitude is put to the test. When there is the loss of someone dear, the loss of wealth, or sickness, one will be more equanimous if one has insight acquired from the teachings in the Abhidhamma. I have witnessed the power of this insight first hand through my contact with several saints and seers. "Why were the saints saints?" someone asked. "Because they were cheerful when it was difficult to be cheerful, and patient when it was difficult to be patient. They pushed on when they wanted to stand still and kept silent when they wanted to talk."[5] The Very Venerable Taungpulu Kaba-Aye Sayadaw of Upper Burma was such a person. Active in body, yet without tension no matter what the situation, he filled every moment and every heart with his peacefulness and compassion.

In the desperate search for peace, seekers after truth are leaving no stone unturned. The conclusion of their efforts is that peace cannot be purchased, but develops gradually as one changes one's attitudes. In their search, many are attracted to the teachings of the Buddha due to their directness, universal suitability, and easy application in daily life. One of the most famous examples given by the Buddha himself is that of the man wounded by a poisonous arrow. The wound will not heal with theory or speculation such as "Who shot the arrow? What is the arrow made of? From which direction did it come?" Only immediate removal of the arrow will cause the wound to heal. So it is with the healing of the mind; only through direct action—meditation and insight—can we cure the mind.

Where does one begin searching for inner peace and harmony? If we just sit down and close our eyes, tranquillity and peace are not likely to appear immediately, but with perseverance based on the aspiration to attain peace, results are guaranteed. Because life is conditioned from moment to moment until our last breath, it is better to engage in spiritual activities whenever the opportunity arises. As the Buddha said to his disciples,, "When you gather together, bhikkhus, you should do either of two things: hold discussion on the Dhamma or maintain noble silence."[6]

The world surely needs the light of Dhamma today. Dhamma teaches the difference between wholesome and unwholesome, virtuous and vicious, good and evil. In this way pain-causing behavior can be avoided and happiness can be cultivated. The Buddha repeatedly preached that this kind of discrimination cannot be acquired through book learning, hence the path of meditation must always accompany the path of study in order to be ultimately efficacious.

The search for happiness never stops. Even in this present advanced age of science and technology, though we have so much comfort and luxury, still the question we ask ourselves is, "Am I happy?" With all our material wealth, we can buy medicine, but not health. We can buy food but not appetite. We can buy a bed but not sleep. Neither intellect nor wealth can give us happiness; it does not come from the outside. We are responsible for finding it within ourselves. I hope that this book will share the unique psychological contributions of the Buddha's path of meditation through the use of contemporary psychological language, and that the insights of Buddhist psychology can help reconcile the dilemmas of modern personal identity. In this way a solid foundation can be laid upon which to set the core question of Buddhist psychology, "Who am I?" I will explore the answers found in the seven books of the Abhidhamma.

1

The Major Features of Abhidhamma and Their Benefits in Daily Life

Numerous books and voluminous commentaries have been written on Buddhism since its early days. The scholars of the East and West, the classical writers, and the commentators have attempted to write on the life of the Buddha, his teachings, and his disciplinary code, according to their own depth of understanding and perspective. Hence, the bulk of authoritative Buddhist literature is vast.

The core of this book is based primarily on the Pali Buddhist literature which pertains specifically to the psychological and ethical aspects of the Buddha's teaching. There will also be reference to some works of historical background on Buddhism, a few parables, and concepts and points of view now current in Western thought. This should help the reader to understand and value the Buddha's teachings.

Thousands of pages of the Buddha's teachings are devoted to a highly systematized compilation known as the *Tipiṭaka*, The Three Baskets, which comprise the earliest Buddhist canonical literature. These three baskets of oral teachings were recited at the Second Council in the 4th century B.C.E. and also at the Third Council in 250 B.C.E. It was in approximately 25 B.C.E. that the Pali canon was first recorded in writing in Sri Lanka. According to the *Mahāvaṃsa* (Sri Lankan Chronicles) the period between 483 B.C.E. and the first century C.E. was marked by constant reinterpretation of the Master's words. Thus, less than 200 years after Buddha's passing, sects began to form.

The Three Baskets of the Pali Canon are known as the *Sutta Piṭaka*, the *Vinaya Piṭaka* and the *Abhidhamma Piṭaka*. The Abhidhamma, or

Basket of Ultimate Things or Truths, is a work of seven volumes; it will be the primary tool by which we investigate and interpret different views of self. The *Abhidhamma Piṭaka* is a work of marvelous complexity and profundity though as reading material it tends to be very dry. It is of primary interest to Buddhist scholars, psychologists, and philosophers, in contrast to the *Sutta Piṭaka* which consists of discursive, easy to read, and quite understandable sermons delivered at different times by the Buddha to individuals or assemblies from different walks of life. All the moral prerequisites for spiritual upliftment are addressed in the *Sutta Piṭaka*. The *Vinaya Piṭaka* deals with an exposition of rules and regulations applicable to the order of monks (*bhikkhu*) and nuns (*bhikkhuni*).

The Abhidhamma quite literally means 'higher' (*abhi*) truths or doctrine (*dhamma*). According to Very Venerable U Thittila Aggamahāpandita, a very reputed scholar and monk of Burma,

> Abhidhamma is a philosophy in as much as it deals with the most general causes and principles of things. It is also an ethical system because it enables one to realize the ultimate goal—*nibbana*. As it deals with the working of the mind, thoughts, and thought processes and psychic factors, it is also a system of psychology.[1]

For a beginner, it is extremely difficult to start with the books of the Abhidhamma without first digesting the *Abhidhammattha Sangaha* known in English as *An Introduction to the Categories of the Abhidhamma Philosophy* written by Anuruddha, an elder teacher who lived during the 11th century C.E. According to Anuruddha, the ordinary states of mind of an individual are full of suffering *(dukkha)* and defilements (*kilesa*). It is through meditation that one passes on to the higher states of consciousness.

The Abhidhamma books that are available seem like recipe books or like catalogs which are comprehensive only for those who are well grounded in Buddhism. To the beginner, such a compressed style will seem meaningless. I will attempt to follow the example of Professor D. Kosambi who wrote The *Butter Commentary* on the *Abhidhammattha Sangaha*. As the name implies, I would like my explanations to be simple, soft like butter and meaningful for the students who desire to study sincerely. In this way, a general knowledge of the Abhidhamma may easily be acquired. I will avoid the original style of cataloging as much as possible so that the reader will be able to go deeply into the teachings and more easily gain a practical realization of the Buddha's message, and I will make every attempt to use layman's language and will use technical terms only when necessary.

The doctrine of Abhidhamma is about ultimate teachings, or ultimate truths. Here, "ultimate" refers to direct experience and not to metaphysics. Thus, Abhidhamma falls within the category of introspective psychology. It is a close and systematic observation of one's own experience which helps one to observe with profound awareness the fluctuating consciousness within. Abhidhamma is an exposition of natural laws of the true nature of reality. It is an analytical explanation of the different nature of physical and mental states. It is the penetrating study of the true nature of mind and matter (*nāma-rūpa*).

The *Abhidhamma Piṭaka* is composed of seven books in which Buddha is said to have expounded the Higher Teaching:

English	Pāli
Classification of dhammas	*Dhammasaṅgini*
Divisions	*Vibhaṅga*
Discussion of the Elements	*Dhātu-kathā*
The Concept of Personality	*Puggalapaññatti*
Points of Controversy	*Kathāvatthu*
The Book of Pairs	*Yamaka*
The Book of Causal Relations	*Paṭṭhāna-pakaraṇa*

The two most important books are the *Dhammasaṅgini* and the *Paṭṭhāna-pakaraṇa*. The *Dhammasaṅgini* is a classification of existence into the ultimate empirical categories: analysis of consciousness (*citta*), mental factors (*cetasikās*), and mentality and materiality (*nāma-rūpa*). In it is found a systematic analysis of aggregates (*khandhas*), bases (*ayātana*), and elements (*dhātu*). The *Paṭṭhāna-pakaraṇa* is the largest volume, comprising six parts. It is often considered the most important. In it is found the system of co-relation (*paṭṭhāna-naya*), one of the four major applications of the theory of dependent origination (*paṭiccasamuppāda*). Its four major applications are:

The Four Noble Truths (*catuya ariyasacca*)
The Twelve-fold Wheel of Becoming (*dvādasabhavacakka*)
The System of Conditional Relations (*paṭṭhāna-nyāṇa*)
The Law of Ethical Reciprocity (*kamma*)

These four are the cardinal teachings of Theravada Buddhism. But the Buddha said that the one who will understand the *paṭiccasamuppāda* will understand the Dhamma. It seems the Buddha prized *paṭiccasamuppāda* very highly. In meditation, he found a method already long practiced, but where many of his contemporaries failed, he succeeded:

"Though only my skin, sinews and bones remain, and my blood and flesh dry up and wither away, yet will I never stir from this seat until I have attained full enlightenment." So indefatigable in effort, so unflagging in his devotion was he, and so resolute to realize Truth and attain full enlightenment.

Applying himself to the "Mindfulness on in-and-out Breathing" the meditation he had developed in his childhood, the Bodhisatta entered upon and dwelt in the first meditative absorption. By gradual stages he entered upon and dwelt in the second, third and the fourth jhanas. Thus cleansing his mind of impurities, with the mind thus composed, he directed it to the knowledge of recollecting past births *(pubbeniva-sanussatinana).* This was the first knowledge attained by him in the first watch of the night (6 p.m. to 10 p.m.) Then the Bodhisatta directed his mind to the knowledge of the disappearing and reappearing of beings of varied forms, in good states of existence, and in states of woe, each faring according to his deeds *(cuti + upapata nana).* This was the second knowledge attained by him in the middle watch of the night (10 p.m. to 2 a.m.). Next he directed his mind to the knowledge of the destruction of the taints *(asavakkhayanana).*

He understood as it really is: This is suffering *(dukkha),* this is the arising of suffering, this is the cessation of suffering, this is the path leading to the cessation of suffering. He understood as it really is: These are the taints *(asavas),* this is the arising of the taints, this is the cessation of the taints, this is the path leading to the cessation of the taints.

Knowing thus, seeing thus, his mind was liberated from the taints: of sense-pleasures *(kamasava),* of becoming *(bhavasava),* and of ignorance *(avijjasava).* When his mind was thus liberated, there came the knowledge: "liberated" and he understood:

Destroyed is birth, the noble life *(brahma cariyam)* has been lived, done is what was to be done, there is no more of this to come (meaning, there is no more continuity of the mind and body, that is, no more becoming, rebirth). This was the third knowledge attained by him in the last watch of the night (2 a.m. to 6 a.m.)

> Thereon he spoke these words of victory: Being myself subject to birth, aging, disease, death, sorrow and defilement; seeing danger in what is subject to these things; seeking the unborn, ongoing, diseaseless, deathless, sorrowless, undefiled, supreme security from bondage—*nibbana*, I attained it (literally, I experienced it). Knowledge and vision arose in me; unshakable is my deliverance of mind. This is the last birth, now there is no more becoming, no more rebirth.[2]

The cornerstone of the teaching is found in this doctrine of causation (*paṭiccasamuppāda*). In the *Mahā-nidāna Sutta* of the *Dīgha Nikāya,* Buddha observes:

> This dependent origination is profound and appears profound. It is through not understanding, not penetrating this doctrine that this generation has become like a tangled ball of string, covered with a blight, tangled like coarse grass, unable to pass beyond states of woe, the ill destiny, ruin and the round of birth-and-death.[3]

The *Paṭṭhāna* is just as important as the *Dhammasaṅgini* but far more complicated, even for an expert Buddhist scholar. "Pa," the prefix, means various and "than" means relation or condition. The *Paṭṭhāna* deals with the 24 modes of causal relations which comprise the essence of the Abhidhamma.

The Abhidhamma is considered by the Theravada tradition to be the original trunk of orthodox Pali Buddhism. Also, it is insisted that the Abhidhamma is the direct teaching of the master himself. Buddhism as practiced in Sri Lanka, Burma (Myanmar), Thailand, and Northeast India is a direct continuation of that tradition. The Abhidhamma offers an impressive systematization of the entire reality concerning humanity's liberation from passion and suffering, and the way to liberation. It deals with actuality under an exclusively psychological and ethical viewpoint with a definite practical purpose.

To sum up, the two most important books that comprise the Abhidhamma are the *Dhammasaṅgani* and the *Paṭṭhāna*. A beginner is likely to get confused at the long lists of psychological and ethical terms coming one after another from the very outset in the *Dhammasaṅgini*. For this Nyananponika Thera states:

> The rather bare and abstract form in which the *Dhammasangini* presents its subject matter, the analysis of mind, should not mislead

> the reader into making him believe that he is confronted with a typical product of late scholastic thought. When, in the course of closer study, he notices the admirable inner consistency of the system, and gradually becomes aware of many of its subtle points and far-reaching implications, he will become convinced that at least the fundamental outlines and the key notes on Abhidhamma psychology must be the result of a profound intuition gained through direct and penetrative introspection.[4]

The *Dhammasaṅgini* generally proceeds analytically, anatomizing and categorizing existence into ultimate constituents, which are based on personal phenomena (*dhamma*). The *Paṭṭhāna* uses the method of synthesis and shows that all these phenomena are related and conditioned. This gigantic and most important work of the *Abhidhamma Piṭaka* deals with conditionality and the dependent nature of all the manifold corporeal and mental phenomena of existence, which in their combinations are known by the conventional name of "I," "it," "person," "world," etc., but which in the ultimate sense are only just passing phenomena, nothing more.[5]

According to the Theravada tradition, the Abhidhamma is the domain proper of the Buddhas (*Buddha-visaya*). This impression will find its confirmation as one progresses in a gradual understanding of the teaching concerned. The initial conception of the Abhidhamma in the Master's mind (*manava desanā*) is traced to the time immediately after the great Enlightenment. It was in the fourth of the seven weeks spent by the master in the surroundings of the Bodhi tree that the Abhidhamma was acquired intuitively. The seven days were called by the teachers of old "The Week of the House of Gems" (*ratana-ghara-sattāha*). The "House of Gems" is indeed a very fitting expression for the sparkling, crystal clear edifice of Abhidhamma thought in which the Buddha dwells during that period.[6]

To be sure, the psycho-ethical aspects of the Buddha's teaching are revealed in many important works. I must mention here the *Dhammapada* because it is more accessible to an ordinary, contemporary audience. The *Dhammapada* is equally popular in Buddhist and non-Buddhist countries and is one of the world's great literary works. The central theme of this small but influential book is that righteous conduct and concentration are more important than fanciful speculation about the transcendent and over-attachment to an ultimately transient world. The timeless appeal of this small book attracts even the modern mind. It is in the *Dhammapada* that the ethical aphorisms of the Buddha are chiefly assembled. According to Ananda Coomeraswamy:

> This book is better known in Europe than any other Buddhist scripture, and has been often translated. It is, indeed, worthy of the notice it has attracted, and of the eulogy of Dr. Oldenberg: 'For the elucidation of Buddhism nothing better could happen than that, at the very outset of Buddhist studies, there should be presented to the student by an auspicious hand the Dhammapada, the most beautiful and richest collection of proverbs, to which anyone who is determined to know Buddhism must over and over again return.[7]

Also, concerning the *Dhammapada*, Dr. Oldenberg says: "The proverbial wisdom of the Dhammapada gives the truest picture of all of Buddhist thought and feeling, how the disciples of Buddha saw in everything earthly the one thing, vanity and decay."[8] The thoughts are expressed in terms of emotion and tend towards themes of transience and present a tragic poignancy which is often lacking in the dialogues of the *Sutta Piṭaka*: "He abused me, he struck me, he overcame me, he robbed me—in those who harbor such thoughts, hatred will never cease."[9] Though the *Dhammapada* is not a part of the *Abhidhamma Piṭaka,* it represents the rich ethical flavor of the Buddha's teaching.

All the teachings of the Buddha can be summed up in one word, "*dhamma,*" which means the teaching which enables one to realize the ultimate truth about existence. The particular books of the Abhidhamma, however, may be quite uninteresting, as Sayadaw U Thittila points out: "Abhidhamma is highly prized by deep thinking students of Buddhist philosophy, but to the average student it seems to be dull and meaningless. The main reason is that it is so extremely subtle in its analysis and technical in treatment that it is very difficult to understand without the guidance of an able teacher."[10] I will attempt to reveal its depth psychology and present its profundity in an easy to understand manner; thus we will find out how helpful the study of Abhidhamma can be in our day to day life.

Medieval Theravada commentators described how the Buddha first preached the teachings of the Abhidhamma:

> [T]radition has it that the sixth Rains Retreat was spent on the Makula Mountain and that during the following year the Twin Marvel was displayed again at Savatthi, after which the Buddha ascended to the Heaven of the Thirty-three gods. There he spent the seventh Rains Retreat expounding the Abhidhamma to deities including the deity who had formerly been his mother. At the end of

> that Rainy Season the descent of the gods took place when the Buddha returned to earth.[11]

This view is still widespread among orthodox Theravada Buddhists but scholars beg to differ. In A.K. Warder's opinion, "Historically, however, it clearly indicates that the Abhidhamma was given final form and put to writing many years after the other two *piṭakas*."[12] David Kalupahana also argues that the *Abhidharmakośa* of the monk Vasubandu was the nucleus from which later theories were elaborated.[13] Theravadins reject this interpretation, insofar as they regard the *Abhidhamma* as the actual teachings of the Buddha, and not mere monkish elaborations. Certainly disagreement and disputes arose due to the discrepancies among different schools, but nevertheless, a great deal was shared in common, from the Buddha's dialogues to the arrangement of topics.

Now that the preliminary groundwork has been laid, we can direct our attention towards illuminating the value and importance of studying Abhidhamma. "Abhidhamma expounds the pure, concentrated essence of the Buddha's profound doctrine. The Dhamma, embodied in the *Sutta Piṭaka* is the conventional teaching (*vohāra desanā*), and the *Abhidhamma* is the ultimate teaching (*paramatthadesanā*)."[14]

> The main difference between the Sutta and the Abhidhamma Pitaka is that in the sutta the doctrines are explained in the words of conventional, simple language, but in the Abhidhamma everything is analyzed and explained in purely philosophical terms true in the absolute sense. Thus, in the sutta, stones are called 'stones,' animals, 'animals' and men, 'men.' But in the Abhidhamma realities of physical and psychical phenomena are described and elucidated.[15]

It is said that the *Abhidhamma Piṭaka* excels the *Sutta Piṭaka*. The reason is that the topics in Abhidhamma are treated and expounded very thoroughly and completely. In the *Aṅguttara Nikāya* of the *Sutta Piṭaka* the discourses of the Five Aggregates (*khandhas*) or personality occupy only a page or two, whereas in the *Puggalapaññati*, the fourth book of the Abhidhamma, the exposition is so meticulously analyzed and explained that at least 175 to 200 pages are written.

> The discourses in the Sutta Piṭaka were generally expounded to suit temperaments of different people and so they are rather like

> prescriptions. In the Abhidhamma Piṭaka all these doctrines are systematically elucidated from the philosophical, psychological and physiological standpoint. As such Abhidhamma is underlying all the teachings of Buddhism. A knowledge of it is therefore essential to understand clearly the Buddhist Doctrine.[16]

From the above standpoints we can say that the *Abhidhamma Piṭaka* can be compared with the whole medical field and the suttas are like prescriptions. The Abhidhamma is very deep and abstruse; it includes an analysis of mind and matter. If we study it properly, our understanding will become sharp and clear. Even the language of Abhidhamma is different as there is no such language as "I," "you," "he," "she," "man," "woman," or a "being."

The Buddha talked about two kinds of truth. Conventional truth (*sammutisacca*) is the truth based on everyday language. When we say, "This is a tree, or a river, or an animal," we are dealing with the world of conventional truth. When we speak of aggregates (*khandhas*) or the combination of mind and matter, then we are talking about ultimate or absolute truth (*paramatthasacca*). Language is created and used by human beings everywhere to communicate or to express things and ideas experienced by their sense organs and their mind. The language used in Abhidhamma describes four ultimate realities: mind (*citta*), mental factors (*cetasikās*), matter (*rūpa*), and the *summum bonum* of Buddhism—*nibbāna*—which can be defined in English as the complete cessation of suffering.

Since Abhidhamma deals with ultimate realities, the language it uses can be said to be very scientific. For example, the terms used in a laboratory are different from the terms used outside the laboratory. In medical terminology, the word "edema" is used to refer to swelling. In the science laboratory, water is referred to as "H_2O," which is its scientific term. In the same way, on a conventional level, we say "person" or" human being" whereas Abhidhamma would say Five Aggregates, 12 Sense Bases, 18 elements, etc. The language used in Abhidhamma, though dry and sterile to many, is highly prized by those who can appreciate the root of Buddha-Dhamma: in this cosmos, nothing is permanent, happiness is elusive, and there is no abiding substance or anything eternal which we can point to. According to Abhidhamma, all phenomena in this world consist of mind and matter. "Mind knows activities such as eating, drinking, going, coming, standing, breathing, etc. It cannot do them by itself. It needs the body (matter). Mind wishes and body does the work or carries out the order of the mind. Mind is like the driver, and the body or matter is like the car."[17]

If the mind is calm and clear, the being concerned feels fresh and vigorous. If the mind is controlled by mindfulness, we will not commit evil deeds, evil speech or entertain evil thoughts, and we will surely be liberated from the painful grasp of all miseries, conflicts, and problems in the world. Abhidhamma deals directly with those elements which not only constitute our personality but our very existence.

A study of the Abhidhamma can be of great value to us in our day to day life, as we will come to know and understand life as a collection of momentary events. Our practice will make clear that our lives exist from moment to moment. The past moments have gone, they cannot be made to come back. They are just memories, and the future is not yet born. Therefore it is a mystery: the present is now and is all that really exists. Abhidhamma helps us to see all the different moments of life, moments of seeing, hearing, smelling, tasting, touching, and thinking. Taste, for example, is different from tasting. Taste is just the matter in the mind-matter process; tasting is the mind.

I will focus on the *Dhammasaṅgini* and *Paṭṭhāna* because a proper understanding of these two books can make our lives as firm as a rock. These two books can have a profound healing effect by bringing us out of the suffocating darkness of ignorance; when one recognizes one's type of temperament, one will also find ways to modify or balance the temperament if necessary, and the inconceivable potentialities latent within us can be developed.

In the *Kanakacchapa Sutta,* the Buddha warned about the difficulty of being reborn as a human being after inhabiting a hell realm through misconduct:

> At one time the Buddha addressed the disciples thus, "There is, O Bhikkhus, in the ocean a turtle, both of whose eyes are blind. He plunges into the water of the unfathomable ocean and swims about incessantly in any direction wherever his head may lead. There is also in the ocean the yoke of a cart which is ceaselessly floating about on the surface of the water, and is carried away in all directions by the tide, current and wind. Thus these two go on throughout an incalculable space of time; perchance it happens that in the course of time the yoke arrives at the precise place and time where and when the turtle lifts up his head, and yokes on to it. Now, O Bhikkhus, is it possible that such a time might come as is said?" "In ordinary truth, O Lord," replied the Bhikkhus, "it is impossible; but time being so vast, and an aeon lasting so long, it may be admitted that perhaps at some time or other it might be possible for

the two to yoke together, as said; if the blind tortoise lives long enough, and the yoke does not tend to rot and break up, before such a coincidence comes to pass."

Then the Buddha said, "O Bhikkhus, the occurrence of such a strange thing is not to be counted a difficult one; for there is still a greater, a harder, a hundred times, a thousand times more difficult thing than this lying hidden from your knowledge. And what is this? It is, O Bhikkhus, the obtaining of the opportunity of becoming a man again by a man who has expired and is reborn in any of the four realms of misery."[18]

So devote your time in study and practice. Why float aimlessly in the ocean of ignorance? Start right away and plunge into meditation; learn to recognize the mistakes which may spoil the harmony in your life. As all of you know, mistakes in social and business life are expensive, but mistakes in the conduct of life are dangerous to life itself. Strive to deepen your understanding about human nature through the practice of meditation. According to Very Venerable Taungpulu Kaba-Aye Sayadaw, we can strengthen our efforts if we take refuge in the Buddha, Dhamma and Saṅgha, also known as the Triple Gem. This initial act of preparation and commitment will reduce timidity and procrastination and thereby enable us to take up practice in a confident way.

A Sri Lankan Maha Thera, Venerable Mirisse Gunasiri, wrote about the value of Abhidhamma in the *Ceylon News* in 1946:

In Burma Abhidhamma is given its due place of honor in monasteries and Buddhist schools. Works on Abhidhamma are annually produced by clergy and laity. Hardly may one come across even a layman who has not studied the fundamentals of this abstruse subject. Even old songs and lullabies are based on points of Abhidhamma.[19]

In the West, scholars and students are becoming very interested in the study of Abhidhamma and are trying their best to find a common meeting point for understanding the problem of self, commonly called "personality." But anyone with average intelligence and interest can profit from studying, and can discover who we are, what we are, and where we are going. In the words of Mrs. Rhys Davids, "Abhidhamma deals with (1) what we find (a) within us (b) around us and of (2) what we aspire to find."[20] Abhidhamma is not a subject for the superficial reader. It is meant for the truth seekers, only those who want to develop insight, and hence it is an indispensable guide for those who are seeking to attain the higher grades of consciousness and also the highest ideal of spiritual life—*nibbāna*.

Now two questions arise, "Is Abhidhamma absolutely essential to realize *nibbāna,* the goal of Buddhism?" and "Is the study of Abhidhamma necessary to understand the ultimate nature of things or the things as they are in a profound way?" The answer to both questions is: yes and no. An understanding of Abhidhamma for one's own deliverance and the realization of truth is not essential, but some people are of intellectual temperament and therefore do not feel satisfied without reading, questioning, and discussing. The realization of truth (*dhamma*) is based on personal experience (*sandiṭṭhika*). So, ultimately, one will have to look within if the truth is to unfold itself. For instance, in the days of the Buddha the nun Patacara, who lost every member of her family, realized *nibbāna* while reflecting on the disappearance of water that washed over her feet. And the disciple Kisa Gotami, who lost her only son, became whole by seeing impermanence while watching the stars fade in the rising dawn. There are many other examples of those who attained sainthood without knowing even a word of Abhidhamma. Today, students are practicing the mindfulness-insight or *satipṭṭthāna-vipassana* method of meditation and are getting much benefit out of it without any formal knowledge of Abhidhamma. Even by watching a fallen, withered leaf, one can attain higher grades of consciousness. "To a profound thinker, a slight indication is sufficient to discover great truths."[21]

The Buddha is said to be a Great Physician. Even as the physician strives to restore health to a sick person, the Buddha tries to restore all of us to our condition of freedom, a condition without greed, ill will, or ignorance. To achieve this, the knowledge of Abhidhamma is very beneficial; it is said the map is not the territory and the territory is not the map, but with the help of the map we may reach our destination with less difficulty. Abhidhamma can help us understand our own character, an essential step on the way to becoming a more complete human being.

Abhidhamma examines the various aspects of the so-called individual or person and analyzes them. We always talk about good, bad, attractive and unattractive qualities in individuals. According to Abhidhamma there is nothing which is absolutely definite and true for everybody, because what is agreeable or desirable to one may be disagreeable or undesirable to another; our sense of what is wholesome and unwholesome develops out of habit. To illustrate this fact, let me relate a story told by Very Venerable Taungpulu Kaba-Aye Sayadaw:

Once there was a golden swan living in the Himalayas surrounded by beautiful flowers and crystal clear streams. He was living on juicy fresh fruit of various kinds. One day the golden swan went exploring to see what the rest of the earth was like. He came to a pond of muddy water where he saw a crane searching for food. Swan felt sad to see such a skinny bird standing in the water, sticking his long beak in the mud. He asked the crane, very sympathetically, "My poor brother, you are so thin and unhappy. What are you doing?" The crane replied, "I am looking for food." The swan inquired again, "What do you eat, my brother?" The crane replied, "Fish." This made Swan very unhappy. "Fish are very smelly and you have to kill them, which is a great violation of disciplines," said Swan. The golden swan tried to convince the crane to eat better food and encouraged him to follow him to the mountain. The crane, after listening and listening, at the end asked, "Does your mountain have muddy water where I can fish?" "No," said Swan, and seeing the dissimilarity in their living habits, gave up all his efforts to dislodge Crane from his home.

Here we see how the sense of appreciation varies from individual to individual resulting in clashes of vision and a clash of judgments among people. Our visions may be covered with illusion, our judgments colored by individual likes and dislikes. We need to practice in order to see the Truth which lies beyond all opinions and interpretations. Abhidhamma is the tool which helps a seeker see that Truth.

Abhidhamma is the penetrating study of the true nature of mind and body. "Tradition attributed the nucleus of the Abhidhamma to the Buddha himself."[23] As a mark of gratitude to his mother, who died seven days after giving him birth and was reborn in a heavenly plane, Buddha preached the Abhidhamma continuously for three months to release her. In Buddhism, heaven is not the final destination. Then he taught it to his disciple the Venerable Sariputta, who is credited with assembling the *Abhidhamma Piṭaka* as we know it today.

As Abhidhamma is so profound, how can one best understand the topics and subject matter of Abhidhamma? One can read all the books of Abhidhamma, all its commentaries, subcommentaries, and can learn to repeat some of the formulas from memory. But if one merely reads, the knowledge of Abhidhamma remains purely theoretical. Bookish knowledge is one thing and experiential knowledge another. Through his insight, the Buddha experienced himself and then taught what he experienced. Hence we need to apply our study of Abhidhamma to a regular meditation practice so that the real understanding of Abhidhamma can emerge.

When we study Abhidhamma, we must understand each topic with respect to the following four aspects (1) by way of characteristic; (2) by way of function; (3) its manifestation; and (4) its proximate cause. Of the four ultimate realities taught in Abhidhamma, one is *nibbāna*. One must understand this reality of *nibbāna*—the supreme state marked by the cessation of suffering—with regard to all these four aspects. Only a practitioner can understand these four aspects, and the practitioner can experience them only through his or her own practice of mindfulness-insight (*satipaṭṭhāna-vipassana*) meditation. Only an *arahat* knows an *arahat*. This is why practice is essential to comprehensive understanding.

Reading Abhidhamma books will certainly help the student become acquainted with long lists of words, but without insight, understanding will be partial. The knowledge of Abhidhamma and the practice of *satipaṭṭhāna-vipassana* meditation go hand in hand. The books represent the maps. When you start your meditation practice, you will be in the territory and will know where you are and what you are seeing, hearing, and so on. At that time, the study of Abhidhamma will be even more clear and profound.

2

Abhidhamma: Comparisons and Contributions to Modern Psychology

The study of Abhidhamma, or Buddhist psychology, has much to contribute to Western psychology. It is claimed in the East that Buddhist psychology is rational, that it has a yardstick of morality, and that it exerts a humanistic influence in the lives of people. Buddhist psychology frees the individual from deep-rooted emotional conflict which results from understanding the self as an isolated entity, separate and alone in a hostile world. By elucidating such principles as interconnectedness, continuity, mutuality, and support, Abhidhamma enhances the sense of self, introducing flexibility and altruism as natural capacities in the psyche which can be cultivated for the happiness of all.

If a thinker wishes to remain on the firm ground of experience and yet postulate an abiding ego, this ego will have to be found within the Five Aggregates (*pañcakkhandha*), or somewhere in the totality of the mental and physical (*nāma-rūpa*) processes of life which these groups represent. The belief in an eternal and abiding self will be challenged as soon as the arising and disappearing of these aggregates has been perceived through meditation. If there is not a real abiding 'self,' then there must be some continuity which transcends intellectual forms and which maintains the continuity of experiential processes. In the Abhidhamma it is the forces of *kamma* which remain active, entirely undisturbed by the disintegration of the physical vehicle.

The insubstantiality of the self has also been discussed in the West. Bertrand Russell comments in his *History of Western Philosophy*:

> What can we know about Mr. Smith? When we look at him, we see a pattern of colors; when we listen to him talking, we hear a series of sounds. We believe that, like us, he has thoughts and feelings. But what is Mr. Smith apart from all these occurrences? A mere imaginary hook from which the occurrences are supposed to hang. They have in fact no need of a hook, no more than the earth needs an elephant to rest upon. Mr. Smith is a collective name for a number of occurrences. If we take it as anything more, it denotes something unknowable.[1]

Those who believe in a soul only too often override the limits set by experience, and concern themselves with something completely unknowable. The Buddha, however, was not a metaphysician, but a sober realist who would not engage in groundless speculations. Buddha's attention was towards a non-intellectual meditative process, what one could call the Wisdom Mode. This may be the reason why the Buddha's teachings have such a powerful appeal to modern seekers.

Born on the full moon day of Kason (May) in the 6th century B.C.E. in Lumbini near the Indian border and Nepal, Gotama's early life was a beautiful one. Of royal parents, he spent his youth in the lap of luxury. But to his gentle heart, the burden and misery of the world, the unintelligible enigma of life became a heavy weight. He keenly felt the transient character of everything in life and longed for a solution, one that would satisfy the deepest problems of existence.

Impressed by the uncertainty of life and urged on by a deep love for humanity, Prince Siddhartha renounced the world. He abandoned his loving wife, his new-born son and the royal throne and became a wandering hermit. Those who did not understand his sacrifice criticized him bitterly as being selfish and negligent towards his wife, son, and father. The grandeur of this step is in accordance with the Eastern ideal of renunciation as the surest way for the attainment of the highest truths. Truth does not reveal itself to the person of culture—it dawns in the heart of the seeker in a rare moment of spiritual insight.

Buddha first tried to know the ultimate truths through philosophical discussion, but subtle philosophic thought did not satisfy him. He therefore took to the life of penance. He practiced austerities for a full six years, but instead of enlightenment he experienced growing weakness and loss of concentration; he became thoroughly convinced of the futility of asceticism. He changed his tactics: he began to eat one meal a day and gradually regained his physical strength. His meditation became stronger with the practice of mindfulness, and with this balanced routine the long sought-for illumination arose in his purified mind. He knew that he had discovered the true solution to the mysteries of life. As Piyadassi Thera related in *The Buddha's Ancient Path:*

> Rigorous have I been in my ascetic discipline. Rigorous have I been beyond all others. Like wasted, withered reeds became all my limbs...' In such words as these in later years, having attained to full enlightenment, did the Buddha give his disciples an awe-inspiring description of his early penances.[2]

Thus did the Bodhisatta Gotama find the sovereign remedy for the ills of humankind; he became a great healer and consummate master-physician (*bhisaka*) known to all as the "Buddha." With this triumph a new chapter in the history of humanity's spiritual endeavor was opened. He now decided to make known this great truth which he had realized with so much difficulty.

When Buddha appeared in the 6th century B.C.E., the world was replete with many fantastic thoughts and speculations. This era was one of the most remarkable in all history, an age of intense intellectual and religious awakening marked by a new quest: transcending discursive thought. It was about the same time that Western civilization, inaugurated by the teaching of the Ionian school and Heraclitus, was giving a new turn to early Greek thought by introducing the principle of universal flux, which explained everything in terms of forces, movement, and dynamic energy. In Heraclitus' words: "You cannot step twice into the same river; for fresh waters are ever flowing in upon you."[3] It was at the same time that Jeremiah was giving a new message to the Jews in Babylon, and Confucius was invigorating the national life of China with his teaching of social ethics. All had transcended the restricted abstract intellectuality and were placed in the ocean of post-intellectual meditative possibility. With the Enlightenment of the Buddha the ancient world was given a new vision, a new evaluation of life, a final solution to the riddle of the universe which was simple, yet fundamental.

In modern times, scientific achievement has revolutionized the way of human life. Probably the most characteristic feature of the modern age is its material progress. Modern men and women, whatever their social condition, expect a higher degree of physical comfort and a greater satisfaction of their material needs than their ancestors did. The machine, with its high productivity, is responsible: there is a never-ending array of luxurious things which money can buy, but can money buy happiness? Or life? Even with so many material possessions, people are not happy. We may possess all kinds of treasurers, but if our higher nature remains obscured we can never be happy.

Different countries in different cultural eras have different psychological problems. At the beginning of the twentieth century, Sigmund Freud responded to cultural pressures by identifying sexual frustrations as the source of all human problems. His younger colleague, Carl Jung, talked about the goal of individuation as the "wholeness" which is represented by the archetype of Self. "Self" here means wholeness, where all factors—thinking, feeling, sensation and intuition—are harmonized.

In the 1920's, Otto Rank wrote that the underlying roots of people's psychological problems at that time were feelings of inferiority, inadequacy and guilt. In the 1930's, the psychological conflict shifted again. Karen Horney pointed out that hostility between individuals and groups was often connected with competitive feelings. In the 1950's Rollo May identified the feeling of "emptiness" as the chief problem of people:

> By that I mean not only that many people do not know what they want; they often do not have any clear idea of what they feel...They have no definite experience of their own desires or wants. Thus they feel swayed this way and that, with painful feelings of powerlessness, because they feel vacuous, empty.[4]

Different psychologists have used different expressions, such as "will to joy," "will to power," "will to wealth," "will for social adjustment," and so on. The school of existentialist thought (not a new phenomenon—many people have traced the roots of existentialism to ancient philosophy) was a kind of revolt against what was perceived to be the meaninglessness of life. It seems that Buddhism finds common ground with the existentialists of contemporary European philosophy and religion. Like the Buddha, for example, Kierkegaard carried on an intense encounter with the reality that can never be spoken.

The high incidence of personality disorders in present day civilization is believed to be a new phenomenon. The increase is due to the insecurity engendered by excessive competition in commerce and industry, the fear of nuclear war, the striving to "keep up" socially and financially with others, the denial of personal importance in society, and the exploitation of the individual in commercial advertising. All these phenomena are characteristic of this age, and each of these factors is doubtless a potential cause of psychological imbalance. But the people of Lord Buddha's time also faced the existential predicament, and it is this predicament—dissatisfactoriness *(dukkha)* and how to eliminate it—that Buddha was interested in. He said, "As the vast ocean, O disciples, has but one taste, the taste of salt, even so this doctrine and discipline has but one taste, the taste of deliverance."[5]

In order to work out a means of deliverance, it is necessary that one should know the true nature of the human being's present existence. The way of life taught by the Buddha is methodical, resting in a meditative sphere, and based on three cardinal characteristics of individual existence: impermanence *(anicca),* unhappiness or suffering *(dukkha),* and egolessness or impersonality *(anattā).* It is within this meditative context that Buddhistic spiritual discipline becomes clearer and more meaningful.

In order to deal with these three characteristics of existence, Buddhism introduces a point of reference which Western psychology has been unable to fit comfortably within its theories: the field of ethical values as fundamental to higher states of concentration and wisdom. Here again it is necessary to clarify certain differences between the Eastern and Western methods of inquiry. The philosophies of the West discuss the different problems of metaphysics, ethics, logic, psychology and epistemology separately from an abstract, speculative perspective; in the East these are treated as one, as so many intellectual abstractions. Though the basic problems of philosophy in the East have been the same as in the West, and the chief solutions have striking similarities, the methods of philosophical inquiry differ.

The study of ethics as a particular discipline which contributes to philosophical inquiry as a whole was due originally to Aristotle. Aristotle maintained that throughout the fundamental dialogues of Socrates and Plato 'virtue is happiness,' a doctrine with which Buddhism would be in agreement. In Buddhism a good person and a happy person are the same: "Happiness is the outcome of good conduct."[6]

According to Professor Abraham Wolf, in the West, "Ethics is not a positive science but a normative science—it is not primarily occupied with the actual character of human conduct but with the ideal."[7] Professor Wolf's statement seems to relate to Abhidhamma philosophy where the supramundane (*lokuttara*) state of continuous concentration (*samādhi*) leads to insightful experience (*pañña*)—which is beyond good and evil. From this point of view, Buddhism can be said to provide a comprehensive approach to ethics and ethical behavior. The Buddha attempted to establish an order based upon moral integrity in a meditative sense, as indicated above. Nowhere did he suggest that anyone should change the world for the better. His idea of improvement was to effect a change in one's own thoughts, speech, and actions and hence one's own attitude toward existence. He always spoke from a psycho-ethical rather than an intellectual perspective.

It is clear that the Buddha gave the religious quest an entirely new orientation, although Buddhism is not just a religion. It is a course that guides a disciple through pure living and pure thinking to the goal of supreme wisdom and deliverance from all evil. It is a gospel of life—a life of love and service, and as such, it can be called a religion. In the spiritual quest, some systems fail to attach proper values to human life on earth. Buddha stressed the beauty and dignity of ordinary life from a post-intellectual meditative perspective.

Buddha was primarily an ethical teacher. When anyone asked Buddha metaphysical questions such as whether the soul was different from the body, whether it survived death, whether the world was finite or infinite, eternal or non-eternal, etc., he avoided discussing them by keeping silence. He considered such questions intellectual abstractions leading away from the path to enlightenment. Searching for solutions to problems for which there is not sufficient evidence leads only to different partial views and conflicting one-sided accounts such as the description of an elephant given by different blind persons who touch its different parts.[8] A person who indulges in speculative practice remains entangled in the net of theories he himself has woven. Instead of discussing metaphysical questions, which are ethically useless and intellectually uncertain, Buddha posed four questions about suffering—its nature, its origin, its cessation, and the path leading to its cessation. The questions and answers have come to be known as the Four Noble Truths (*cattari-ariya-sacca*). They are (1) life in this world is full of suffering (*dukkha sacca*); (2) there is a cause of this suffering, which is craving (*dukkha-samudaya sacca*); (3) it is possible to stop suffering through the cessation of craving (*dukkha-nirodha sacca);* and (4) there is an eightfold path which leads to the cessation of suffering (*dukkha-nirodha-magga sacca*). The Four Noble Truths form the central conception of Buddhism and originate from a non-discursive meditative perspective. Buddha proclaimed for the sake of all human beings the principles on which he had conducted his research so that all who wished to do so could follow his methods and know the final truth themselves.

Because the Buddha's way is the way of rationality, he did not ask for absolute faith in himself or his teachings. Rather, as he instructed the Kalama clan:

> It is proper for you, Kalamas, to doubt, to be uncertain...Do not go upon what has been acquired by repeated hearing; nor upon tradition, nor upon rumor; nor upon what is in a scripture; nor upon surmise; nor upon an axiom...nor upon another's seeming ability; nor upon the consideration, 'The monk is our teacher.' Kalamas,

> when you yourselves know: These things are bad; these things are shameable; undertaken and observed, these things lead to harm and ill, abandon them...Kalamas, when you yourselves know: These things are good; these things are not blameable...undertaken and observed, these things lead to benefit and happiness, enter on and abide in them.[9]

The most important barrier to an understanding of Buddhism among Western people is the tendency to take Buddhism as an interpretation of life, another system or doctrine, or a group of teachings about self, suffering, and *nibbāna*. This is an obstacle because no system of thought and no understanding of a theoretical nature can communicate the distinctive features of Buddhism. Once Buddha said that the mere reading and studying of medical textbooks never cured any man's disease. For that cure one has to take medicine. In this and many other ways the Buddha stressed that his system was practical and not theoretical.[10] It is practical in that it provides a way, a path in the post-intellectual direction, and allows for decision-making without haunting speculative obsessiveness.

The West, because of its affection for the theoretical, reaches for the philosophical or psychological doctrines in Buddhism, leaving the deeper implications of Buddha's teaching untouched. Western readers have numerous books available to them on the central conceptions, the Monastic Order, the Four Noble Truths, the Eightfold Path, the doctrine of the Three Characteristics of existence, the concept of *nibbāna,* and the doctrines of *saṁsāra* and *kamma.* But the Buddhistic insights concerning the incommunicable pinch of experience have yet to win a major audience in the West. In the West, one understands something when it has been given a name, been framed in a theory, and had its truth or falsity listed in devised, experimental situations. Buddhism, on the other hand, has to be understood on completely personal and practical grounds.

The Buddha's teachings are deeply and discretely concerned with truth and the pragmatic importance of things more than with theories. Everything he taught seems to have had practical bearing upon some concrete quest and struggle. As the renowned psychologist William James comments: "Essential truth [in this case, the general Buddhist doctrine], the truth of the intellectualists, the truth with no one thinking it, is like the coat that fits though no one has ever tried it on, like the music that no ear has listened to."[11] The Buddha would have appreciated James' distinction between "knowledge about" and "acquaintance with."

William James was extremely interested in the varied expressions of spiritual and religious experience, including those reflecting Buddhist ideas and beliefs. He wrote about them at length in his famous book *The Varieties of Religious Experience*. He comments:

> I am ignorant of Buddhism and speak under correction, and merely in order the better to describe my general point of view; but as I apprehend the Buddhistic doctrine of Karma, I agree in principle with that. All supernaturalists admit that facts are under the judgment of higher law; but for Buddhism as I interpret it, and for religion generally so far as it remains unweakened by transcendentalistic metaphysics, the word 'judgment' here means no such bare academic verdict or platonic appreciation as it means in Vedanta or modern absolutist systems; it carries, on the contrary, *execution* with it, is *in rebus* as well as *post rem*, and operates causally as partial factor in the total fact.[12]

William James more than anyone else had the courage to challenge the firmly established paradigm of reason and science. James' vision gave ample encouragement to America, the adolescent nation, to pursue the truth and act. It seems James realized that the intellect devoid of feeling is bound to misrepresent the world. James, as a pragmatic thinker, realized that thinking loses itself in pure abstraction. He emphasized the need for truth to be practical. Two thousand six hundred years ago the Buddha's emphasis was also practical; he never wanted to answer abstract questions as he felt they were not helpful at all.

I have wondered many times whether these two opposite ends of the world—the East and the West—will ever understand each other, so it is significant to see that the dialogue between Buddhist psychology and Western psychology has recently received serious attention. This dialogue is contributing an entirely new chapter to the East-West encounter, and ending once and for all the long isolation.

Abhidhamma prompts an arduous type of spiritual experimentation. The techniques given in Buddhist psychology are used to deal with the anxiety-producing tensions of life. Accordingly, "Real Buddhism is found on the non-cognitive and non-discursive cutting edge of experience. No one can win his way by gaining more knowledge about the steps that must be taken. Discussion gets one no where at all. Each must work out his own salvation with diligence."[13]

Interest in Buddhism in the West began in earnest in 1881 with the founding of the Pali Text Society in London by T.W. Rhys Davids and his wife, Mrs. C. Rhys Davids. Another wave started in America in 1875 when Madam Blavatsky and Henry Olcott founded The Theosophical Society, and after a short time Mr. Olcott founded the Buddhist Theosophical Society in Madras, India.[14]

Early in the 20th century, D.T. Suzuki, a brilliant student of Zen Master Sogen Shaku, created a great deal of interest in Zen Buddhism. The seeds that were planted by the Zen Masters have influenced America since World War II. The explosion of interest in higher grades of consciousness and meditation practice for spiritual development also contributed to the birth of transpersonal psychology. Carl Jung was exceedingly knowledgeable about Eastern psychologies. Of course, he states very openly that his trip to India in 1938, "was not taken on my own initiative. It arose out of an invitation from the British government of India to take part in the celebrations connected with the twenty-fifth anniversary of the University of Calcutta."[15] He prepared himself for this journey by reading about Indian philosophy and became convinced of the deep value of oriental wisdom. At the same time he cautioned:

> The historic development of our Western mentality cannot be compared in any way with the Indian. Anyone who believes that he can simply take over Eastern forms of thought is uprooting himself, for they do not express our Western past but remain bloodless intellectual concepts that strike no chord in our inmost being.[16]

I feel that Jung tried to explain Eastern practices and their experiences in his own terms from a limited understanding of Eastern disciplines. Jung warned Europeans against over-involvement with Eastern practices even though he cautiously engaged in them himself. In his autobiography he writes:

> I was frequently so wrought up that I had to do certain yoga exercises in order to hold my emotions in check. But since it was my purpose to know what was going on within myself, I would do these exercises only until I had calmed myself enough to resume my work with the unconscious.[17]

As his remark implies, Jung's primary purpose was not to investigate higher grades of consciousness as defined in Buddhism. Nevertheless, although not supportive of Eastern theories, Carl Jung's analytic model has extended the West's public consciousness of the contributions of non-Western systems of thought.

On the other hand, Erich Fromm counted Buddhism as one of the five major influences in the development of his thoughts and views. Erich Fromm was a Zen meditator and also quite familiar with the *Abhidhamma Piṭaka*. Fromm contributed greatly to the study of Abhidhamma through his writings on the relationship between psychoanalysis and Zen Buddhism.

I cannot fail to mention Abraham Maslow, who in his earlier years moved in the direction of Aldous Huxley, who postulated that "the core religious experience is shared by all the great world religions, Buddhism among them."[18] In his later years, Maslow's views gradually expanded. Just before his death he wrote:

> I consider Humanistic, Third Force psychology, to be transitional, a preparation for a still 'higher' Fourth Force psychology, transpersonal, transhuman, centered in the cosmos rather than in human needs and interests, going beyond humanness, identity, self-actualization, and the like.[19]

The aforesaid statement opened the door for transpersonal psychology where Buddhist psychology, Eastern psychology, and meditation practices would follow afterwards. Twentieth century Western psychology started to acknowledge the ancient wisdom and techniques of Buddhist psychology. Suddenly, experiences that for centuries had appeared to many Westerners as nonsensical or pathological became valid and valued in the lives of a sizable minority. Western culture has never been the same since.[20]

According to Abhidhamma our real problems can be solved by giving up false concepts and fixed ideas which hinder our ability to experience happiness and peace. The direction of modern society, if it continues, will inhibit or even destroy our ability to achieve mental balance and tranquillity. While science and technology have made life comfortable, they have also distracted our attention from the world within. As the Buddha says, we human beings are mysterious and have inconceivable potentialities; we need to explore our creative capacities, which include saintly characteristics as well as criminal tendencies.

Freudian psychology underestimated human possibility and saw no real means for the cessation of suffering. Buddhist psychology posits infinite possibility and offers the alternative of transforming the mundane consciousness into supramundane consciousness. Through the practice of meditation, the Buddhist paradigm transforms *bhavacakka*—the Wheel of Birth—into *dhammacakka*—the Wheel of Truth. Buddhahood is attained by transforming ordinary states of consciousness, principally through meditation, and once attained,

Buddhahood is characterized by the extinction of all those states, e.g., anxiety, needfulness, pride, which pin one to the ordinary realms of existence. The Buddhist order of development is a progressive detachment from discursive thinking through the meditative process, the results of which lie beyond the reach of contemporary psychology.[21]

Abraham Maslow as a founding father of both humanistic and transpersonal psychology studied human experience and helped people become psychologically healthy through the achievement of "Peak experiences," defined as "brief but extremely intense, blissful, meaningful and beneficial."[22] Similar experiences, for example *jhāna,* (absorption or trance) are also recognized in Buddhist psychology, even though they are not the goal. As the Buddha says, "Though one conquers in battle a thousand times a thousand men, yet he is the greatest conqueror who conquers himself."[23]

The intricate workings of the human mind are more fully dealt with in the *Abhidhamma Piṭaka* than in any other system of speculative thought. The problems of the West lie in a conceptual-empirical tendency to rely solely on psychological, material knowledge, or scientific and technological knowledge which does not solve the deeper problem of living in this world. Science and technology sometimes lead to a multiplication of problems. The West has also turned to drugs as a way to answer mental frustrations.

> Psychedelics also had a powerful impact and unleashed an unprecedented range and intensity of experiences on a society ill-equipped to assimilate them. For the first time in history, a significant proportion of the culture experiences alternate states of consciousness. Some of these were clearly painful and problematic.[24]

Drugs are definitely no substitute for true meditation and yoga. Taking drugs can expand your experience of consciousness, but this is not the same as attaining insight through an unaided expansion of consciousness.

There are a few outstanding figures whose names and contributions to the understanding of Abhidhamma can never be forgotten so long as the word "Buddhism" lives on. It is important to mention the names of the Western Buddhists such as Ananda Metteyya (Allan Gueth) who was ordained in Burma in 1901. Also, Venerable Nyanatiloka, a German born monk who contributed to the translation of the *Aṅguttara Nikāya*. He also resided in Burma many years and then returned to Sri Lanka in 1906. Venerable Nyanatiloka founded a monastery in Sri Lanka and named it "The Island Hermitage." He retired after his work as the Buddhist Publication Society's chief editor of Pali to English translation. At present, Bhikkhu Bodhi, an American bhikkhu, is in charge of Buddhist Publication Society.

I feel that both Buddhist and Western psychologies are still unfolding. Buddhist psychology or Abhidhamma is much older than Western psychology, yet there is a deep interconnectedness between the two. If we keep the Buddha's Middle Path, Buddhism will survive in the West. The two extremes of indulgence and rigidity will have to be avoided if the real identity of Buddhism is to be kept up. Both extremes have the danger of losing the authenticity of the Master's teaching. The spread of Buddhism in the West is slow, and Fedor Stcherbatsky's remarks made seventy years ago are still applicable today: "Although a hundred years have elapsed since the scientific study of Buddhism has been initiated in Europe, we are nevertheless still in the dark about the fundamental teachings of this religion and philosophy."[25]

The dominant drive of Western culture to organize itself under the demands of a theoretical system has prevented an understanding of the entire scope of the teachings of Buddha. According to the Buddha, craving is the source of the ills and misery of human existence. Everything the human mind anticipates, remembers, or grasps in cognition can be the source of human suffering. The order of life which appears so substantial is just illusion. Deliverance from clinging to forms of organization, whether human or divine, is the keynote of Buddhist striving.

A great deal of investigation has taken place over the centuries regarding the Path, the Way, and the Dhamma. Buddhism cannot be understood if it is seen as an interpretation of life; rather, it is an effective method of dealing with the anxiety-producing tensions of life. It is accomplished by following several steps: becoming accustomed to a simple way of life, practicing moralities, and attaining a state of mindfulness and awareness. There must be a strenuous effort to overcome, at least temporarily, sensual desire (*kāmacchanda*), ill-will and anger (*vyāpāda*), sloth and torpor (*thīna-middha*), restlessness and worry (*uddhacca-kukkucca*), and doubt (*vicikicca*). These are the Five Hindrances (*pañcanivaraṇa*) to mental development and vision, and having subdued them the meditator will feel very happy. When the Five Hindrances are suspended, the body becomes extremely calm and a special feeling of joy arises. In such a state of happiness, the mind is able to achieve much concentration.

Buddhism briefly defines meritorious and demeritorious volition (*cetanā*) as *kamma*. Buddha said: "Volition, O monks, I declare is *kamma*...Having willed, man acts by deed, word, or thought."[26] The expressions "good karma" and "bad karma" used frequently in the West, are meaningful remarks, therefore, only insofar as they relate to kammic activity which is either profitable and wholesome (*kusala*) or unprofitable and unwholesome (*akusala*). The notion of fate, here, does not apply.

The Buddha repeatedly exhorted his disciples to give up wrong views concerning the nature of self. The relation between kammic forces and the Three Characteristics is indicated in the *Poṭṭhapāda Sutta:*

> There are, Potthapada, some *samanas* and *brahmanas* who hold and expound the view: certainly the self is completely happy and healthy after death. I went to them and said: 'Venerable sirs, I have heard that you teach the certainty of a happy and healthy self after death. Is this so?' They acknowledged that it was so. I asked: 'Is the world, as you know it and see it, completely happy?' 'No,' they said. I asked them: 'Have you produced for yourselves complete happiness one night or one day, or even for half a night or half a day?' Then I asked: 'Do you venerable sirs know a path or a method by which a realm of complete happiness may be reached?[27]

Such wishful thinking and speculation may be compared to the person who falls in love with a place or person he has never seen. As H. Saddhatissa relates: "If then we have no details of the state of happiness, other than that it is 'happy,' it remains only to consider what things give rise to unhappiness and avoid them. Hence the Buddha's teaching of the Four Noble Truths: 'Suffering, the origin of Suffering, the Cessation of Suffering, and the Way to the Cessation of Suffering."[38]

The Buddha wittily remarked that holding to a wrong view of self "is like building a staircase for maintaining a palace which one has never seen."[39] "Cut out the love of self as you would an autumn lily with the hand. Cherish the path to peace, to *nirvāna,* pointed out by the Buddha."[30] Within Buddhism there is no other axiom for the attainment of peace other than liberation. There are differences as well as affinities between the teaching of the Buddha and those of some of the West's noted thinkers, particularly in the line of Heraclitus, James, Whitehead, and Russell. All were exponents of process philosophy—advocates of freedom from intellectual abstractions because impermanence is the law of life.

The doctrine of non-self (*anattā*) is a cardinal tenet of Buddhism and the one that distinguishes it from all other religious systems, including Hinduism. Ever since the time of Aristotle, the "soul" or animus—which is supposed to enter the body at birth and permeate its substance—has been taken as the entelechy of being in Western thought. Buddhism denies the existence of any such entity. Every state of consciousness can be postulated without reference to any persisting ego-principle which is an intellectual abstraction, holding fast to a concept, a so-called ultimate. Like the body (*rūpa*), the mind (*nāma*) is a succession of states, a causally-conditioned continuum whose factors are sensation (*vedanā*), perception (*saññā*), volition (*saṅkhāra*), and consciousness (*viññāṇa*), all complex psychic conditions prohibiting any simple analysis. Introspective examination of the states of the mind (*cetasikās*) in order to realize this truth is one of the exercises which is meditative. In the words of Nyanaponika Thera, "In the methodical meditative practice, the contemplation of the State of Mind will help to assess one's progress or failures (e.g., of mental concentration or not)."[31]

The understanding of the Buddhist principles of impermanence, suffering as being the product of craving, (*tanhā*), and non-ego, if accomplished without attachment to a fixed theoretical process, brings about a re-orientation of mind towards a progressive meditative continuum which is characterized by psychological stability and moral awareness. But Buddhism points out that this is not an effect which can be obtained by theoretical means or exercises of the intellect alone. Rather, it is the result of an inner effort, beginning with and sustained by the exercise of will. There must first of all be the desire to put an end to suffering; then different techniques of meditation (*bhāvanā*) are used according to the personality of the meditator. They are prescribed by the teacher just as treatment is given by a psychiatrist; the mode of treatment is selected with an eye to the requirements of the patient.

Here it should be pointed out that Buddhist teachings do not encourage repression of natural desires. Once such desires are forced below the surface of consciousness, they are liable to grow into morbid obsessions, breaking out in hysteria or manic-depressive symptoms. Buddhism does not favor this rough treatment of the psyche for it produces so many undesirable results. Instead, Buddhism employs simple awareness and discipline or admission or acceptance of their presence with the suggestion to slowly defuse their intensity. Thus, the mind's basic propensity toward craving *(tanhā)* in general, and its speculative propensity towards the attainment of higher psychic pursuits *(iddhi)* gives way to a sensitized and awakened encounter with the world, one which is balanced and reverent.

Buddha fully justified his ethical disciplines by going beyond the progressive processes of *śīla* and *samādhi* to the enlightening states of insight inherent in *paññā*. To aid the progress of the aspirant, Buddha preferred a highly rational approach: our thoughts should be confined to this world as perceived in the reality of the present moment, and to the improvement of our existence by progressive concentrations. It may be called Phenomenalism insofar as Buddha taught that we are sure of the phenomena, only not as it is, but as breeding the psychic condition of sorrow (*dukkha*). It is, therefore, also a kind of Empiricism in method, because experience according to Buddha is the source of knowledge manifesting as psychic transformation which leads to dispassion and ultimately *nibbāna*. Above all, Buddhism is a discipline of one's psyche in its totality—through meditative practices which free one from addiction to a theoretic approach. It is but natural then that Buddha gave a pre-eminent position to the mind when he said:

> Mind is the forerunner of (all evil) states. Mind is chief; mind-made are they. If one speaks or acts with wicked mind, because of that, suffering follows one, even as the wheel follows the hoof of the ox that draws the cart.
>
> Mind is the forerunner of (all good) states. Mind is chief, mind-made are they. If one speaks or acts with pure mind, because of that, happiness follows one, even as one's shadow that never leaves.[32]

3

Personality in Abhidhamma

This chapter grew out of a discourse by my most revered teacher, the Very Venerable Taungpulu Sayadaw on the topic of *nāma-rūpa* (mentality and materiality). Many people have been impressed, amused and fascinated with his direct and simplified version of this foundational teachlng. I intend to undertake a presentation of the personality from the perspective of Abhidhamma. The emphasis will be on the process of understanding "who I am and what I am." No one fully understand what life is, although as organisms, we all possess it. For the most part, the fact of life is simply taken for granted. As science progresses, more questions are raised than are answered, and we have no real understanding of the fundamental forces and, correspondingly, no idea of life's ultimate potential.

Our outlook as human beings is rooted in the brain, central nervous system, and structure of the body. The brain provides the basis for the processing of sensory information, the forming of concepts, and for our participation in both base and sublime emotions. The nervous system is the avenue or gateway to the surrounding environment. By means of it, we are able not only to detect what is going on in the world, but also to respond appropriately. The location of the eyes at the front of the head permits stereoscopic vision. As a result, we have greater depth perception than we would otherwise, and can concentrate on a single object. We possess hands with opposing thumbs allowing us not only to grasp both large and small objects, but also to perform delicate and creative tasks such as microsurgery and piano sonatas. With an erect torso, we are in a position to overcome obstacles in our path and move toward the horizon. All of these various facets work jointly to shape our unique outlook as a species; collectively, they provide a unique anatomical basis for our liberation.

Each of us has some concept of himself or herself as a person capable of mobilizing intention and desires. Language is the expression of thought and provides both a map of how we represent our world to ourselves and a primary means for others to gain access to our thoughts. An examination of the way in which we think about ourselves, therefore, is linked to the way in which we speak about ourselves. This examination will be useful in gaining access to the larger question, "Who or what am I?"

We refer to ourselves and to each other in a variety of ways everyday. We say, "Today I feel great," or "I saw your new house," or "I have lived here before," or "Tomorrow I will be in New York." None of us who has learned the language has the slightest difficulty in making statements of this sort. Even some philosophers have been tempted to say we have hit the ground of certainty. So when the Buddha asserts that there is no "I" or no "self," we may find this puzzling and frustrating because he appears to be saying what is contrary to our perception and the world and our place in it. The solid ground seems to vanish into thin air.

In modern Western philosophy, the so-called "linguistic turn" represents a differing approach to the resolution of certain kinds of perennial shifts. The movement known as logical positivism grew up in a rarified atmosphere[1] and came about as a reaction against the speculative excesses and abstruseness of 19th century and early 20th century philosophy in order to resolve certain problems in the physical and social sciences. It insisted on the marriage of meaning and verification. A method of analysis was used based on Descartes' *Discourse on Method* and Newton's *Rules of Reasoning in Philosophy,* among other sources. It attempted to get rid of philosophy as aesthetics, ethics and metaphysics—whatever was devoid of cognitive meaning. While the enterprise as a whole did not succeed, it helped to shape the development of behavioral psychology.

The use of language is also important; if we examine the suttas we discover what seems to be a distinction between two epistemological orders of experience, that is, conventional (*sammuti sacca*) and absolute truth (*paramattha sacca*). Upon close examination, we notice that no clear-cut distinction is ever made between them. There is only a distinction between two kinds of discourses: those of direct (*nitathana*) and those of indirect (*ñeyyattha*) meaning.[2] Buddha did not give answers to some questions, as he intended to show that sometimes our questions themselves make no sense and using language as a heuristic device for quieting discursive propensities only reinforces the illusion of personality.

From the perspective of Buddhist psychology, a person is ultimately only mind and matter (*nāma-rūpa*), or the totality of five aggregates (*khandhas*), namely, feeling, perception, volition, consciousness and matter. Therefore, an individual or person is seen as a collection of different parts, and there is no need to cling to a personal identity. On the level of conventional truth (*sammuti sacca*) one will continue to speak of person, personality, I, mine, etc. Yet the goal of understanding "self" is to develop the right understanding of one's own personality or temperament in order to lead a balanced and harmonious life.

In the Pali canonical literature, as well as in the commentaries, the famous book *The Questions of King Milinda*—an inspiring dialogue between King Milinda and the monk Venerable Nagasena—stands alone in its original and entertaining approach to the topic of personal identity. The King asked Bhante Nagasena, "is a person just born that person himself, or is he someone else?" "He is neither that person," said the elder, "nor is he someone else."[3]

From that answer a series of questions and answers develops, which arrives at the conclusion: "...one element perishes, another arises, succeeding each other, as it were, instantaneously. Therefore neither as the same nor as a different person do you arrive at your latest aggregation of consciousness."[4] King Milinda accepts this explanation and understands that within the individual there is no personal identity but only an ever-changing phenomenon which has the appearance of continuity.

This phenomenon is analyzed into its component parts as mind and matter in the *Abhidhamma Piṭaka*. From the perspective of ultimate truth (*paramattha sacca*), the individual (*puggala*) is seen exclusively as a combination of the five aggregates, or *khandha*. In addition, the conditions contributing to the origin of personality (e.g., conditional relations, *kamma* and rebirth), are discussed. "Being" or "person" is seen as concept.

The *Puggala Paññatti* classifies individuals according to their ethical qualities. A similar style can be found in several of the suttas, namely, the *Saṅgiti Sutta* and some parts of the *Aṅguttara Nikāya* of the *Sutta Piṭaka*. In the ultimate sense, with the transformation of the belief in personal identity one enters the stages of sainthood and finally *nibbana*, the ultimate goal of Buddhism.

In the *Sutta Piṭaka,* which is the collection of discourses of the Buddha, where the analysis of the Abhidhamma is presented in conventional language, "the stone" is called the stone and "the person" is called the person. The suttas also import necessary information about how one can change unwholesome personality traits to wholesome ones. Through meditation and by the practice of the triadic principle of virtue (*sīla*), concentration (*samādhi*), and wisdom (*pañña*), different types of personality can be developed into the supramundane ideal or enlightened personality.

In Buddhist psychology, no static entity, no everlasting self or soul, is found. Hence, Buddhist psychology is dynamic in its approach and outlook. In the three signs of existence (*ti-lakkhana*), the true nature of all component things is reflected. That which is of the nature to arise is also of the nature to cease (*anicca*). There is coming and going, forming and breaking, arising and passing away. There is only the continuous process of change; nothing can be found that will last forever. As there is no lasting entity, there also cannot be an everlasting soul or self (*attā*). As the *Dhammapada* says, *"Sabbe saṅkhāra anicca, Sabbe saṅkhāra dukkha, Sabbe dhamma anattā,"*[5] which means, "All conditioned things are transitory, all conditioned things are painful, all elements are without abiding essence." These three salient characteristics of every object not only inspired me to go into these profound and valuable teachings of the Buddha, but also opened a new avenue to explore and examine who is this mysterious "I, me, mine."

The *Sutta Piṭaka* contains stories and parables which can be understood easily by the reader. The understanding they provide to the mystery of "I, me, mine," is necessary but not sufficient. It is the *Abhidhamma Piṭaka* which analyzes and explains the teaching of the Buddha in purely psychological terms, which are true in an absolute sense. Before going into the definition of person and personality according to Abhidhamma, it is important to give a brief explanation of how these terms are commonly used and understood in Western psychology.

"Person" is described as an individual human being (man, woman, or child), as distinct from a thing or an animal. The concept of person further includes the actual physical body, as distinct from clothing or from the mind and soul. "Person" also describes that body with its clothing and adornment, as presented to the sight of others. The meaning also includes the actual self or being of a man or woman, and leads thus to the understanding of personality or individuality of a human being. Personality is personal identity. It is also "that quality or assemblage of qualities which makes a person what he is, as distinct from other persons; a distinctive personal or individual character especially when of marked or notable kind."[6]

In philosophy, "person" is defined as a self-conscious or rational being, and the quality of personality is known because of perception. Johansson points out that Western psychology is mainly concerned with the sense organs and the nervous system. Mind and the conscious processes are difficult to study objectively. He says, "It has become the fashion in Western psychology to avoid them and study only the corresponding behavior."[7]

To clarify the terms "person" and "personality" according to Theravada Buddhism, I will give an explanation of person and personality (a) on the conventional level (as presented in the *Sutta Piṭaka*), and (b) in the ultimate sense (as analyzed in the *Abhidhamma*).

The Pali word *puggala* means the person or individual; its synonyms include personality, individuality, being, or self. It stands for all those terms designating a personal entity. In the translation of the *Puggala Paññatti*, B.C. Law followed Childer's definition of *puggala* as "an individual or a person, as opposed to a multitude or class, a creature, a being, a man."[8]

The term "personality" has not been explained or defined in the *Puggala Paññatti* itself, and it may be assumed that "person" and "personality" are used as synonyms. George Grimm defines personality from the Pali word *sakkaya* which means *sat*, being, and *kāyā*, or summary of the five groups. Therefore, the summary of the five groups is defined as the real being.[9] Johansson defines personality as "recurring processes of a certain type."[10]

According to Buddhist psychology, all those terms designating a personal entity are mere names, conventional modes of expression (*vohāra-vacana*). The *Sutta Piṭaka* uses them as such so as to not misapprehend them.

In Buddhist psychology the answer to the query, "Who am I?" and "What am I?" is always given by enumerating the five aggregates. It is said that the combination of these five aggregates is what is called a being, person, or personality.

> "Personality, personality, is said, Venerable One; but what is personality, does the Blessed One say?" Thus, the adherent Visakha asked the sage nun Dhammadinna, his former wife. "The five groups of grasping are personality: that is the grasping-group of the corporeal form, the grasping-group of sensation, the grasping-group of perception, the grasping-group of the activities of the mind, the grasping-group of cognition. These five groups of grasping, friend Visakha, constitute the personality, so the Blessed One said.[11]

What are these five aggregates? They are (1) matter (*rūpakhandha*), (2) feeling (*vedanākhandha*), (3) perception (*saññākhandha*), (4) mental formation (*saṅkhārakhandha*), and (5) consciousness (*viññāna-khandha*). These five aggregates can be classified into two categories, namely, mind and matter, or mentality and materiality. Of these five components, feeling, perception, mental formations, and consciousness constitute mentality, mind.

The first of these five aggregates is matter (*rūpa*). Matter is composed of the four great primary elements: earth, water, fire and air, also known as solidity, fluidity, motion, and temperature, and of the four secondary elements of color, smell, taste, and nutriment. These eight elements are inseparable.

Solidity (*pathavi*) is the element of expansion. Because of this element of expansion, objects occupy space. Its hardness, rigidity, and compactness gives it a supportive function.

Fluidity (*apo*) is the element of cohesion. It has the function of binding which keeps matter from being scattered.

The element of motion (*vāyo*) represents the restless and dynamic aspect of matter.

The element of heat or temperature (*tejo*) is the element which matures, intensifies, or imparts heat to the other three primaries. This element also includes cold, as "coldness" is a temperature of lower degree. "The aggregate of matter includes the whole realm of physical substance, both in one's body and in the external world."[12]

The second aggregate is that of feeling or sensation. The feelings, which can be pleasant, unpleasant or neutral, arise dependent upon contact of one of the six sense organs with an object. It is the function of the third aggregate of perception to recognize the objects of the mental and physical world. In accordance with the six sense organs (eye, ear, nose, tongue, body, and mind) and their corresponding sense objects (visual, auditory, smell, taste, touch, ideation), perceptions are six-fold. These perceptions, the third aggregate, if not guarded by mindfulness, lead to mental formations (*saṅkhārakhandha*), expressed as cravings or aversions. These desires have inherent within them the tendency to be fulfilled. Here the volitional action—the *kamma* producing action—starts.

The fifth aggregate is consciousness (*viññāṇakhandha*). It is the most important one. Consciousness has the six sense organs as its basis, and the corresponding external phenomena as its object. Consciousness does not recognize an object, rather it is the awareness of the presence of an object. It is through the third aggregate—perception—that objects can be recognized. But consciousness depends on matter, feeling, perception, and mental formation, and cannot exist without them. These five aggregates combined constitute the person, I, self, or being. Apart from these there is no lasting entity, and there is nothing extra which exists separately from these aggregates.

In the *Questions of King Milinda*, the Venerable Nagasena discusses the idea that a person or being can be likened to a chariot. Only when all the parts are combined in a correct manner can one speak of a chariot. In the same manner, if the five aggregates come together, one speaks of a being.[13] The famous chariot illustration in the conversation of the Arahat Nagasena and King Milinda elucidates the significance of the Five Aggregate theory by explaining the functions and limitations of conventional language. The word "chariot" is but a mode of expression for axles, wheels, chariot-body, pole, and other constituent members, placed in a certain relation to each other. But when we examine the members one by one, we discover that no one part taken by itself can be called "chariot." Likewise, not one of the aggregates represents the I, or the ego, or self. Only when all the parts come together does one get the idea of I, mine, or person. But this idea is only one of the 52 mental formations of the fourth aggregate, namely the idea of self (*sakkaya diṭṭhi*). And as the Venerable Nyanaponika states in *The Heart of Buddhist Meditation,* "...person, individual, I, mine, man, woman, is the deepest and most obstinate delusion in us."[14]

According to the Abhidhamma, person or individual is defined as psycho-physical phenomena (*nāma-rūpa*). In the Abhidhamma one cannot find words of conventional language such as man, woman, animal, house, sun, moon, etc. These names are all concepts, which have been established for the purpose of communication to distinguish one thing from the other. They have no meaning in a real or ultimate sense. "By viewing 'name and form' in the light of being, a person takes what is impermanent as permanent. Why? Because being or person is nothing but a concept."[15]

In the conventional sense, *nāma* is divided in the four-fold division of the aggregates, as already presented in the earlier part of this chapter. On the other hand, *rūpa* designates the material form, or body, which is the basis of personality. *Nama* or mind has a very specific meaning in the Abhidhamma. Mind is the awareness of an object, animate or inanimate. Mind is perceived as a powerful force. Mind is the healer, mind is the slayer. Mind, though not intellectual, is intelligible; its quality is like space—shining, clear, and empty.

Mind is studied and analyzed in the Abhidhamma in a very microscopic and meticulous way. There are different grades of mind. Mind can be wholesome or unwholesome, superior or inferior, conscious or unconscious. Mind is described as a dynamic continuum. Mind can be compared to a stream. This dynamic continuum is not limited to one life span. It is the dynamic force of the past, present, and future. Because of this continuum through the past, present, and future, one is interested in one's mind and personality, as the mind is responsible for all the bodily, verbal, or mental activities—whether wholesome, unwholesome, or neutral. The entire study of the Abhidhamma is for the purpose of developing and uplifting the mental states, so one can live a happier, more harmonious, and more peaceful life. Therefore, in order to progress spiritually, one first needs to develop one's mind.

Besides the mind, a person or individual has the physical body, which is only matter. Matter is one of the five aggregates which has been described as the combination of the Four Great Primaries (*mahā-bhūtas*) in the earlier part of this chapter. Mind and body are interrelated. The mind knows activities such as eating, drinking, standing, walking, breathing, etc. But it cannot do them by itself. To perform these functions the mind needs the body.

The Very Venerable Taungpulu Kaba-Aye Sayadaw gave a very clear analogy concerning the relation of mind and body. He compared the physical body to a car, and the mind to a driver. The car cannot run without the driver starting it. Unless the mind wants to do something, the body cannot do anything.

> The wish to go is the mind,
> The thing that goes is the matter.
> The thing that goes is not
> a person, a being,
> neither man, nor woman,
> nor soul, nor ego.
> Only mind-and-matter goes;
> Only mind-and-matter goes.[16]

From this it is clear that the mind is the leader of all activities. Therefore, if the mind is dull, the being concerned is weak; if the mind is clear and pure, the being concerned is vigorous and clear. If the mind is controlled by mindfulness, one will no longer commit unwholesome deeds, and the being concerned surely will be liberated from suffering. In the words of the Venerable Sayadaw, "If mind-and-matter be discriminately recognized and realized, the yogi does not cling to the view of personal attachment (*sakkaya diṭṭhi*) but abandons it; and thus gains the purity of views (*diṭṭhi visuddhi*)."[17]

The Abhidhamma emphasizes the process of continual transformation both in the body and in the mind. The body is a collection of sensation, vibration and movement, and in the mind there is a continual flow of phenomena, thought, moods, images, and emotions. Both mind and body are in a constant flux. There is nothing one can hold on to. There can arise from this insight a feeling of insecurity, despair, and even disgust. But with the progress and development of the mind, one will be able to get rid of fear, frustration, and confusion.

If one can understand and accept change, then one will be able to live in harmony with the seasons of life. Can one stop the process of aging and decay of the body? Can one stop the disintegration of mind? Instead of fighting this universal law of change, if one can understand this process deeply, one will be able to live fully in the present moment. Grief, lamentation, despair, and pain will be tempered by wisdom. Of course, to attain this spiritual wisdom one must pursue the difficult but not impossible process of "letting go."

It is easy to appreciate the pragmatic approach and practicality of Buddhism. As Johansson says, "Buddhism never had a reason to work out a complete and scientific theory of personality. The purpose was intensely practical."[18] Because of this, I will formulate a few criteria for identifying one's personality according to Theravada Buddhism. To achieve lasting transformation, one needs to know the inherent and latent tendencies of the personality, and how to tackle certain aspects which may appear unexpectedly. It is by introspection through the meditative process that one can achieve right understanding. In order to do so, honesty with oneself, enduring patience, and persistent effort are necessary conditions.

For this study, a classification of psycho-ethical standards has been developed which can be used as a basis for the understanding of human nature. According to Buddhist psychology, traits of personality can be viewed as wholesome (*kusala*), unwholesome (*akusala*), and neutral (*kiriya*). From the ethical point of view they can be described as inferior and superior, and from a religious perspective as mundane and supramundane.

What are these wholesome, unwholesome, and neutral personality traits? From the Abhidhamma point of view, the healthy personality is one whose actions are neither harmful to oneself nor to others. These actions produce good and wholesome results. These actions are morally good and blameless; they cause harmonious and peaceful living. There are three doors through which we act in the world, namely, the body door, the speech door, and the mind door. When performing any action, one has to be attentive and conscious in order to root the action in a mental state of non-greed (*alobha*), non-hatred (*adosa*), or non-delusion (*amoha*).

Unwholesome actions are all those actions performed bodily, verbally or mentally which are harmful to oneself or others. All unwholesome actions are said to have their main root in ignorance (*avijjā*) because the person does not have the right understanding of the consequences of these actions. In addition, these actions are either performed out of greed (*lobha*) or out of hatred (*dosa*).

In the *Puggala-paññatti,* there is an example of what is meant by good and bad. The following questions are asked: "What sort of person is not a good man?" "What sort of person is more 'not a good man' than the 'not good man'?" "What sort of person is 'a good man'?" "What sort of person is a better man than 'the good man'?"[19]

The answer is given with reference to the Five Precepts, the basic code of moral conduct in Buddhism. The "not good man" will not keep the precepts or higher conducts. The "more not good man" than the "not good man" will not keep the precepts but also will encourage others not to keep them. The "good man" is one who observes these basic rules of conduct, and the one who is "better than the good man" also encourages others to do so.

The inoperative or neutral actions are all those actions which do not have any result (*kamma vipāka*). These are all the activities performed by the *arahat,* in whom the fires of greed, hatred, and delusion have been extinguished. Even rebirth in the happiest plane of existence under the most favorable circumstances is still another rebirth in the world. Inherent in rebirth is the possibility to return to the lower levels including the animal world, the world of demons, the world of ghosts or the human world. To understand the differences among people—why some are born rich and others poor, why some are healthy, others unhealthy, why some are happy, others unhappy, why some are knowledgeable, others are stupid, why some are pretty, others ugly—one needs to understand the workings of the Law of Kamma. It is through their deeds that individuals are different. The Law of Kamma is profound and is considered a natural law. In Buddhist psychology the emphasis is on its dynamic aspects, pointing out the opportunities for change by one's own effort. The Law of Kamma knows no exceptions and yet it is by no means deterministic.

Although it is not possible to escape the consequences of one's own deeds, whether wholesome or unwholesome, there is still every chance for change. The conditions in this present existence are the result of previous deeds. This body is considered the "old deed," made of past *kammic* actions. Likewise the present activities (wholesome and unwholesome) will be the conditions for future existence. Not all the *kamma* ripens in the present existence, and one is fortunate when one can feel the consequences of a harmful action in this present life. This means that the *kamma* of that particular unwholesome action ripened in this lifetime and will not be carried on into future existences.

The Buddha himself addressed this issue when he instructed the monk Venerable Angulimala. Before becoming a monk, Angulimala had been under the influence of a wrong teacher who instructed him to kill people, collect their fingers, and wear them as a garland. Even though he took the robes of the Buddha's order, he still had to experience the consequences of his previous evil deeds. Once, while going for alms, the Venerable Angulimala was attacked violently and returned from his begging smeared with blood. With a broken almsbowl and his robes torn, he returned to the monastery. Lord Buddha saw him and advised, "Bear it, brahman! Bear it, brahman! You are experiencing here and now the results of deeds because of which you might have been tortured in hell for many years, for many hundreds of years, for many thousands of years."[20] Just as in this lifetime one suffers the consequences of past deeds, in this lifetime one also accumulates the kammic forces for future existences.

The teaching of the Buddha provides a fundamental ethical code. The Buddha not only speaks about suffering, dissatisfactoriness, or pain, he also shows the way to cessation of pain, and the way to achieve the cessation of pain, which is the Eightfold Noble Path. Beginning with proper conduct or common moralities (*sīla*), the Five Precepts lay the foundation for the development of concentration (*samādhi*) and wisdom (*pañña*). It is said, "As hand washes hand and foot washes foot, so morality is purified by wisdom, and wisdom is purified by morality."[21]

The ethics of Buddhism include a concept of responsibility. According to the Law of Kamma, one is responsible for one's own action. This responsibility is accepted if one tries to transform the unwholesome action into wholesome ones. This is achieved by observing the Five Precepts: "To abstain from evil, to do good is the function of *sīla,* the code of conduct taught in Buddhism. *Sīla* embraces love, modesty, tolerance, pity, charity, and happiness at the success of others, and so forth."[22]

From the ethical point of view, one has either an inferior or a superior personality. An inferior person is one who does not keep even the minimal code of conduct found in the Five Precepts; one whose mind is deluded, associates with evil companions, is a drunkard, a gambler, a person of violence, is lazy, does not work on the grounds that it is too hot, too cold, too late, too early, that he has eaten too much or is very hungry. That is, this person not only does nothing, he fails to put forth the maximum effort to accomplish what needs to get accomplished. The superior personality is qualified by taking Refuge in the Buddha, Dhamma, and Saṅgha, by observing higher disciplines, and by being generous, free from stinginess, and of lovely disposition. Established in virtuous conduct, the superior person more easily develops concentration, which leads to wisdom.

This classification does not mean that one is at all times inferior or at all times superior. If the principles are not kept up, it is not difficult to lose them. As the *Dhammapada* says, "Do not disregard evil, saying, 'It will not come nigh unto me;' by the falling of drops even a water jar is filled; likewise the fool, gathering little by little, fills himself with evil."[23] The following stanza deals with the opposite by stating, "Think not lightly of good," and it continues, "Do not disregard merit, saying, 'It will not come high unto me; by the falling drops even a water jar is filled, likewise the wise man, gathering little by little, fills himself with good."[24]

The Five Precepts are by no means commandments. One is not responsible to any external agency or god, nor does one observe the Precepts out of fear of punishment. The observance of the Five Precepts is an act of responsibility, to purify one's own mind, and therefore purify one's speech and action. Doing this leads to a harmonious and peaceful lifestyle, the superior lifestyle. The formula used in the Buddhist commitment to virtuous living shows clearly the intention of taking responsibility for oneself.

> I undertake the precept to abstain from the taking of life.
> I undertake the precept not to take that which is not given.
> I undertake the precept to abstain from abuse of the senses.
> I undertake the precept to abstain from false speech.
> I undertake the precept to abstain from intoxicating drinks or drugs.[25]

The basic moral behaviors are the first stepping stone in the Buddhist way of life. They are based on love and compassion and, if observed sincerely, result in the accumulation of wholesome forces over life times (*pārami*). If one has accumulated enough virtue, then the development of the superior personality is possible. In the *Puggala Paññatti* this process is expressed as follows:

> What sort of person is capable of progress? The persons who are not covered with the veil of karma, not covered with the veil of evil passions, not covered with the veil of the consequences (thereof), who have faith, who have desire, are wise, capable of walking along what is recognized to be the true path in regard to things that are good: These persons are said to be capable of progress.[26]
>
> For this progress one must be firmly established in *sila*. It is the basis for the purification of mind. The precepts are just the means and not the end. They are essential conditions for the attainment of Higher States.[27]

The next step is the development of concentration (*samādhi*). By mastering the mind, one will get the right knowledge (*pañña*). The development of these factors of *sīla, samādhi,* and *pañña* constitutes the process of transformation from the inferior to the superior personality. The inferior personality and the superior personality are still mundane *(lokiya)* personalities. Liable to rebirth in the lower planes of existence, they are unstable. Only the transcendence of the belief in personality as a fixed entity can lead to continuous rebirth in higher planes; such a person possesses a supramundane (*lokuttara*) state of mind.

What is the mundane personality? The mundane personality is still attached to worldly affairs, obsessed by them, and overwhelmed by excitement, sensuous desires, clinging, and craving for existence. On this level one strives for worldly positions, for the acquisition of titles and degrees, for power, property; one works toward the attainment of rebirth as a noble and highly placed human being. Though one may practice *sīla, samādhi,* and *pañña* occasionally, the practice is still directed toward worldly gain, and therefore it is temporary and unstable *(aniyata).*

The Venerable Ledi Sayadaw of Burma compares these achievements with the raindrops falling in an ocean of hot embers: "Just as the heat of embers absorbs the rain drops and makes them disappear, so does the great kingdom of Personality-Belief absorb the Worldings' acts of Morality, Concentration and Wisdom and makes them disappear."[28]

Only if the practice of *sīla, samādhi,* and *pañña* is directed toward the ending of the rounds of rebirth with *nibbāna* as the goal is one progressing from the mundane to the supramundane. The supramundane personality is characterized by its stability and unemotionality. The supramundane personality can be compared to the river. As the river always flows in one direction toward the great ocean, so does the supramundane personality progress toward the great freedom (*nibbāna*). Once the stream-entry (*sotāpatti*) is achieved, there is no chance for a relapse. The overcoming of doubts, wrong belief in rites and rituals, and wrong belief in personality are stepping stones on the way to entering the stream. An individual who has accomplished these steps is firmly on the Noble Eightfold Path. Therefore the moral perfections of thought, speech and action are taken for granted, and unwholesome activities no longer occur. As Dr. Radhakrishnan summarizes this process in the *Dhammapada*: "The Noble Eightfold Path of the Buddha is the best psycho-physical method for human perfection. It is by advancing step by step along the ancient path that one reaches the goal: freedom. One cannot attain freedom all at once."[29]

Freedom here is not external freedom, but internal freedom from impurities, which are also called defilements. Real freedom is the freedom from clinging to personality belief. That is, to have a healthy mind is the result of correct insight into the nature of personality. It is the right understanding of the three signs of existence: change, (*anicca*), dissatisfactoriness (*dukkha*), and impersonality (*anattā*). At this stage the practice of *sīla, samādhi,* and *pañña* is compared to the raindrops which fall into a great lake and stay there as part of the lake.

The distinct characteristics of the human personality according to Buddhist psychology are the three fires of greed (*lobha*), hatred (*dosa*), and delusion (*moha*). They are present in all human beings. Some persons may be dominated by greed, others by hatred or by delusion. But until one has achieved the final liberation, no one is completely free from these fires. They are the very core of every being, and only through continued effort will one be able to transform these obstacles. There are ways to extinguish these three fires. If one can get rid of these fires, one can develop the higher states of consciousness for the betterment of one's life. This is difficult but not impossible. One needs to develop iron will and transparent honesty along with enduring patience and persistent effort to be able to overcome the grip of greed, hatred, and delusion. In Abhidhamma the wholesome states of mind include moral shame and moral dread, as distinct from pathological guilt and worry, both of which can be a big hindrance to spiritual development. We human beings have our desires, taints, biases, etc. We can destroy these by entering upon the Path. Thus the world of spiritual progress consists of desires on one side and their elimination on the other; this understanding is of central importance in the dynamics of personality study.

During his last visit to the United States in 1985, the Very Venerable Taungpulu Sayadaw of Burma taught a meditation aimed at overcoming these three great fires of greed, hatred, and delusion.[30] The meditation consists of the repetition of the following phrases: *"Rāga kinne, dosa kinne, moha kinne."* This means, "Getting rid of lust, getting rid of hatred, getting rid of delusion." Truly, it is easier said than done. This verse condenses the entire spiritual effort into one compact phrase. By repeating it, the practitioner gradually penetrates the meaning. The first stage of practice is to acknowledge the presence of the three fires—the fires of greed, the fires of hatred, and the fires of delusion. Then, after acknowledging them, one must develop the will to get rid of them. We were always reminded by the Sayadaw not to identify with them as *my* greed, *my* hatred, or *my* delusion, or to consider that *I* am getting rid of *my* greed, *I* am getting rid of *my* hatred, *I* am getting rid of *my* delusion. The Venerable Taungpulu Sayadaw said that we can penetrate into the understanding of *anattā* by recognizing that neither greed nor hatred nor delusion are the real *I* or *mine*; simply recognize the presence of these fires. The benefit of this profound meditation is that with the repetition of these words (like a mantra) one's mind slowly abandons greed, hatred, delusion, and gains a happier, lighter outlook. How is this possible? Because at the very moment of concentrating on the phrase no unwholesome activity, whether mental, verbal, or physical, can be performed. Therefore, the chanting of this phrase is also a protection from producing new unwholesome *kamma*; simultaneously it increases wholesome activities, as it is a form of being mindful of wholesome mental activities.

In Buddhist psychology the analysis of personality is undertaken not with any theoretical interest in mind, but for the purpose of evolving a rationale for practical and ethical living. The ideal personality in Buddhism is the worthy one, the perfect one. The final product of Buddhist personality development in Theravada is the *arahat*. The *arahat* is one who has eradicated the defilements, who has lived life for the sole purpose of purification, who has done what was to be done. The *arahat* is the one who has laid down the burden and broken the chain of becoming by getting rid of the five hindrances and the ten fetters. The term *arahant* or *arahat* means the one who has killed the enemy ('ari' = enemy, + 'hant' = to kill). These enemies are the three great fires of greed, hatred and delusion. By getting rid of these fires the *arahat* has turned the Wheel of Existence (*bhava-cakka*) into the Wheel of Truth (*dhamma-cakka*).

In search for this final liberation (*nibbāna*), for peace and happiness, one needs to transform the worldly self into the developed self. This transformation can be achieved by treading on the Noble Eightfold Path; by seeing things as they really are and not as they appear to be; by living a disciplined life; by seeing cause and effect; by overcoming the Five Hindrances (*nivaraṇa*) and destroying the Ten Fetters (*saṁyojana*).

This Eightfold Noble Path constitutes the Fourth Noble Truth (*ariya sacca*), namely, the path leading to the extinction of suffering. The process is gradual: one can attain the four stages of sainthood with its two aspects: (a) entering the path consciousness (*magga*); and (b) attaining the fruit consciousness (*phala*). The four stages of sainthood represent the Four Noble Personalities (*ariya puggala*): (1) stream-winner (*sotāpanna*); (2) once-returner (*sakadāgāmi*); (3) never-returner (*anāgāmi*); and (4) the enlightened one (*arahat*). As one progresses on this path, one will be able to destroy the ten fetters: wrong belief in personal identity (*sakkaya-diṭṭhi*), doubt (*vicikiccha*), wrong belief in rites and rituals (*sīlābbata-parāmasa*), sensuous desire (*rāga*), ill-will (*dosa*), attachment to material existence (*rūpa-rāga*), attachment to immaterial life (*arūpa-rāga*), pride (*māna*), distraction (*uddhacca*), and ignorance (*avijjā*).[31]

Some of these fetters will have to be weakened first before they can be destroyed. To enter the path of the streamwinner (*sotāpañña*), one will have to take a step and enter the stream. Even in this stage, the ups and downs of life appear. The *Puggala Paññatti* gives a very detailed description of this process. Under the heading, "The Stream," beginning with the description of "How is a person who is once drowned just drowned," and ending with "What sort of person is one conforming to faith," 14 steps are described until one can safely reach the other shore, attaining the fruition. Each paragraph emphasizes that unwholesome tendencies and ignorance lead one to being drowned, whereas a virtuous life, faithfully and skillfully lived, will bring one closer to the safe and secured grounds, which is the attainment of arahatship. Of the ten fetters, the streamwinner has gotten rid of the first three, namely wrong belief in personal identity, doubt, and wrong belief in rites and rituals. The *Puggala Paññatti* describes the streamwinner as follows:

> What sort of person is he who undergoes rebirth (not more than) seven times?
>
> Here a person, having completely destroyed the three fetters, becomes a 'stream-attainer'; he is no more liable to fall into a woeful state, but is destined to succeed and has enlightenment as his final end (or aim); running on and transmigrating seven times amongst devas and people makes an end of suffering. Such a person is said to be one not undergoing rebirth more than seven times.[32]

The fruit is attained by knowing that these fetters have been destroyed. The streamwinner is also called the "unshaken recluse," as the *Aṅguttara Nikāya* mentions: "Herein a monk, by wearing out of three fetters is a streamwinner, of a nature not to go to the downfall, one assured, bound for enlightenment. Thus, monks, is a person an unshaken recluse."[33] The next step is taken by weakening the fetters of sensuous desire and ill-will. Again, the knowing of having weakened these fetters signifies the attainment of the second path and fruit stages, the stage of once-returner. This person is compared to a blue lotus recluse: "Herein a monk, by utterly wearing out three fetters and by weakening lust, anger and delusion, is a once-returner. Coming back just once more to this world he makes an end of ill. Thus, monks, is a person a blue lotus recluse."[34]

Getting rid of these two fetters of sensuous desire and ill-will marks the achievement of the stage of the never-returner. Thus entering the path of the never-returner, the knowing of having entered the path and having destroyed the five lower fetters, marks the achievement of the fruit of the *anagami*. Through the removal of these five fetters, rebirth into the lower worlds as animals, ghosts, etc., can be eliminated. This stage is compared to the "white lotus recluse."[35] The remaining five higher fetters of attachment to material life, attachment to immaterial life, pride, distraction, and ignorance, can only be overcome while entering the path of arahatship: "Herein a monk, by the destruction of the *asavas* reaches the heart's release, the release by wisdom, that is free from the *asavas*...and abides therein. Thus is a person a recluse exquisite among recluses."[36]

The "Description by One" in the *Puggala Paññatti* gives a very valid classification for these stages of sainthood by stating: "What sort of person is a learner? The four persons who possess the path and the three persons who possess the fruition are learners. Arahants are non-learners; the remaining persons are neither learners nor non-learners."[37] Having entered the path of arahatship, one strives for the realization of the fruition stage. In the *Puggala Paññatti* it is said:

> A person working for putting away attachment to form and the formless, to pride, haughtiness, and ignorance without any residuum is one working for the fruition stage of arahatship. The person whose attachment to form and the formless, to pride, haughtiness and ignorance has been entirely put away is said to be an arahant.[38]

On many occasions the Very Venerable Taungpulu Kaba-Aye Sayadaw gave an inspiring illustration to explain the stages of sainthood. He compares the four stages of sainthood to holding a star ruby in one's palm. A heavy rainstorm is blowing, and there is darkness. Suddenly, there is a flash of lightning, and one can see for a moment the sparkling of the ruby. Again one is overcome by darkness and rain. Again, lightning flashes and one can glimpse the ruby for the second time. There is repetition of the same for the third time. With the fourth lightning bolt, the darkness is broken. The ruby in one's palm is no longer hidden. Its beauty is now revealed to the purified mind. This is the achievement of the arahatship, the final enlightenment. The successive lightnings mark the attainment of streamwinner, once-returner, and never-returner. The Venerable Sayadaw ends this story by encouraging his disciples to practice mindfulness meditation firmly in order to overcome the darkness of ignorance and to try to see the star ruby at least once.[39]

Therefore, *nibbāna* is a state where greed, hatred, and delusion have been completely extinguished. *Nibbāna* has no location; it indicates the end of the journey, the cessation of becoming, the end of suffering.

Once *nibbāna* is reached, it cannot be lost; it is permanent, stable. It is the fourth of the Four Ultimate Realities (the other three being mind, mental factors, and materiality).

The detailed analysis of personality in the Abhidhamma is not undertaken out of theoretical interest but instead for evolving a rationale for practical living. If everything is arising and passing away, then there is no enduring reality corresponding to the notion of "I," "me," or "mine," which people cling to so strongly.

> In the Tibetan tradition, according to the Buddhist scholar Robert Thurman, the best time to observe the self clearly is when we are in a state of *injured innocence,* when we have been insulted and think, "How could she do this to me? I don't deserve to be treated that way." It is in this state, he says, that the "hard nut" of the self is best found, and the self cannot be truly understood from a Buddhist perspective until it is seen clearly as it appears.[40]

Realization of no-personality in Buddhism implies a realization of transcendental self, absolute self, or *nibbāna.* As the *Dhammapada* teaches:

> I have run through the rounds of countless births, seeking but not finding the builder of this house. Sorrowful, indeed, is birth again and again.
>
> Oh house builder! You have been seen, you shall not build the house again. All your rafters have been broken, your ridge pole shattered. Mind has attained to unconditional freedom with the extinction of desire.[41]

The whole of Buddhist psychology is contained in these two most important verses. What was the Buddha seeking? What has been broken? What has been shattered? The Buddha tells us he has been freed from the sorrowful consequences of repeated birth and death. Hence, the Buddha wanted his fellow beings to understand the no-self doctrine and get rid of chronic craving. But, he said, it cannot be achieved without practice.

4

Causation and Co-relation

During my college days in Rangoon I attended the Venerable U Narada's *Paṭṭhāna* School. One evening I met U Posa of the Burma Civil Service, a renowned Buddhist scholar who I knew well. He was not only a scholar but a very generous and compassionate man as well. He, like a father, addressed me as *thami* (daughter) and said: "Even Lord Buddha enjoined his disciples to meditate in order to experience that all things mental and physical are always in a state of flux. Hence, the Buddha proposed to explain as to how things mental and physical are causally related to one another." Further, he said that as I was taking lessons with Venerable U Narada, the best teacher in the field of *Paṭṭhāna*, I should write a book on the teaching of *paṭṭhāna* in a very simple and non-technical language. This book should be enjoyed by everyone, because once you have an understanding of how all of life is interrelated, you feel much lighter and happier. He stressed that one will have to experience that all things in the world have causes and are causally related to one another, and that there is not a single thing, mental or physical, that is absolutely alone and not related to something else. He gave me the example of how the great ocean gives joy to the fishes, crabs, and other animals who depend on it by way of "non-separation" (one of the 24 Co-relations). He emphasized that the 24 Co-relations must be studied very thoroughly; in addition to memorizing their names, one must meditate on their meanings and chant their names out loud. According to Very Venerable Taungpulu Sayadaw, reciting these 24 Co-relations is a powerful protection against the attack of demons, wild beasts, ghosts; reciting the Co-relations will also bring healing to many kinds of diseases. U Posa concluded our visit by saying: "N + R = O; N – R = D. Are these equations close to *nibbāna* in any way?" He responded to my puzzled laugh by telling me that these equations may have a very deep meaning but without meditating one will not be able to penetrate to the profound truth they represent. Our chance meeting was a true blessing for me as it threw new light on the *paṭṭhāna* with which I was struggling, and I was determined to follow his advice.

One day as I was ardently trying to memorize the 24 Co-relations, another *Abhidhamma* teacher, Venerable Thazi Sayadaw, scolded me by calling me a frog. "The lotus is right on the head of the frog, and all the bees are sucking away the honey, while you are just sitting, watching and croaking." At the time the Very Venerable Taungpulu Sayadaw was residing in our house, and Thazi Sayadaw, one of his closest associates, brought the analogy home: Sayadaw, master meditator and teacher, was like the lotus, and the visitors were like the bees sucking the honey while I just observed the scene, not caring to participate.

"You have croaked enough," said Thazi Sayadaw. "Now go to Sayadaw and ask for his blessing so you can start writing." For such a Herculean task I did indeed receive blessings, and I began my fledgling efforts to reveal the jewel-like insights of the largest book in the *Abhidhamma Piṭaka*.

The starting point of Buddhism is reasoning and understanding. To seekers after Truth the Buddha says do not believe in anything on mere hearsay. Do not believe in anything just because it is the tradition, just because it is old and has been handed down through generations; do not believe in anything simply because the written testimony of some ancient sage is shown to you; do not believe in anything based on the mere authority of your teacher or priests. Depend on your own experience, and investigate yourself. Whatever agrees with your reason and is conducive to your own well-being and to that of all other living beings, accept that as truth and live accordingly.

It seems that Buddhism is the doctrine of actuality, a means of deliverance. It is called *Dhamma* or the Truth, the law which exists in the heart and mind. It is the principle of righteousness. Take an illustration of two persons who meet financial disaster. One reacts emotionally, loses all hope and sinks in health, vigor, and resolution, or he kills himself to end it all. The other man, who has learned to think over the problems of life, to mediate, to rationalize, applies every available method to overcome the problem and finds a satisfactory solution for he has exercised his mind just as the athlete exercises his muscles. He is the master, while the other is the slave. Many disappointments and breakdowns would not exist if people were to live according to the *Dhamma*.

Buddhism is a psychology of help and of attainment of deliverance from unhappiness and suffering. The Buddha explained that however humble or lowly one may be, there is a grain of worth, a little goodness, a spark of wisdom which one can kindle into a flame by conscious human effort. The Buddha encouraged everyone to strive for spiritual development, declaring that every right effort is sure of a reward here and now, in this life, or a future one. The Buddha laid stress on human dignity and taught the worth of the human being. As I have already mentioned, the word of the Buddha is called *Dhamma*, the law of righteousness, that exists not only in the heart and mind but in the universe also. All the universe is an embodiment of *Dhamma*. If the moon rises and sets, it is because of *Dhamma*, for *Dhamma* is that law within the universe which makes matter act in the ways studied in physics, chemistry, zoology, botany, and astronomy. If one lives by *Dhamma*, one will escape misery and come to *nibbāna*, the final release from suffering.

The Buddha taught everyone to rely on themselves in order to achieve deliverance and not to look to any external savior. He never puts himself forward as a mediator between us and our final deliverance, but he can tell us what to do because he has done it himself and so knows the way. However, unless we ourselves act, the Buddha cannot take us to our goal. He can point out the way and he can tell us of the difficulties and of the beauties which we shall find as we tread the way; but he cannot tread it for us.

The life process of the universe is governed by the natural law of cause and effect. The cause ever becomes the effect and the effect ever becomes the cause; so birth is followed by death and death on the other hand is followed by birth. Birth and death are the two phases of the same life process. In this circle of cause and effect a first beginning is not discoverable. According to Buddhism the universe evolved, but it did not evolve out of nothingness. It evolved out of the dispersed matter of a previous universe and when this universe is dissolved, its dispersed matter or its residual energy which is continuously renewing itself, will in time give rise to another universe in the same way. The life process of the universe is therefore cyclic and continuous.

In the heart of every human being there is a spark of wisdom which is ordinarily crippled by selfish desire, hatred, and ignorance, and the purpose of human life is to grow from small to great, from ignorance to enlightenment and from imperfection to perfection. The Buddha also proclaimed that every low desire, every unworthy feeling that we conquer and trample down, and every difficulty we meet with righteousness become rungs in the ladder by which we can climb toward a nobler, higher life. This is the law of *progressive development,* the Buddhist doctrine of evolution, of attainment, of accomplishment. The Buddha drew for us the picture of progressive existence, a growth from small to great, from less to more, from ignorance to knowledge, of development depending upon inward strength, diligence and effort put forth from life to life. This is the doctrine of human perfection won through altruism, discipline, and wisdom. Thus, the material and mental forces combine and re-combine with no underlying substance to make them permanent, and this process, this wheel of life, this "becoming" continues indefinitely until its main cause, craving or selfish desire, is totally eradicated. It is this craving, this selfish desire that sets the wheel of life in motion. The wheel of life is produced by action which is, in reality, volition. The volitional action responsible for the creation of being is called *kamma*. *Kamma* means all kinds of intentional actions, whether mental, verbal or physical; that is all thoughts, words, and deeds. Every action produces an effect. It is cause first and effect afterwards: like tree and shade.

We therefore may say that *kamma* is the law of cause and effect, that each of us is the heir of our deeds and the architect of our destiny. *Kamma,* however, is not determinism nor an excuse for fatalism. The past influences the present, but it does not dominate it. The past is the background against which life goes on from moment to moment, and the past, together with the present, influences the future. But one should remember that only the present moment exists. The responsibility for using the present moment for good or ill lies with each individual, so if one does a good deed or utters a good word or thinks a good thought, the effect upon him will be to increase the tendencies of goodness in him. The practice of good *kamma*, when fully developed, will enable one to overcome evil and thus reach the goal, *nibbāna*.

At the root of all our trouble is our primal state of ignorance, and from ignorance comes desire which sets the *kamma* force in motion. One can ascend to *nibbāna* through the Eightfold Noble Path which we can divide into three: the path of bodily discipline, mental purification, and wisdom. These three divisions can be summed up by one verse of the Buddha's: "To refrain from evil, to do what is good, to cleanse one's mind." This is the teaching of all the Buddhas.

The Buddha is a great benefactor of humanity because he taught people that there is no need for them to look outside themselves to any superior being for help to reach the higher condition of mind and heart possible for them. He pulled everyone to their feet with his gospel of self-help and asked them to go forward by their own strength toward the goal. What does Buddhism mean for the ordinary person going about their work in the world? The Buddha again and again reminded his followers that there is no one, either in a heaven or on earth, who can help them or free them from the results of their past deeds. It is the mind which is enough to guide man in the present and shape his future and bring him eventually to the truth.

Many people in the West as well as in the East think that Buddha's teaching is pessimistic; others think it is optimistic. On the contrary, the Buddha's right view of life is the middle way between two extremes. To understand the causes and the conditions of life one must understand the doctrine of kamma. The doctrine of kamma is neither fatalism nor is it a doctrine of predeterminism. *Kamma* is one of the twenty-four causal relations mentioned in the "*Paṭṭhāna*," one of the seven books in the *Abhidhamma Piṭaka*. The *Paṭṭhāna* describes in detail the various causal relations which govern the whole universe. The twenty-four causal relations are: root, object, predominance, contiguity, immediacy, co-nascence, mutuality, dependence, powerful dependence, post occurrence, repetition, ethical reciprocity, effect, nutriment, control, absorption, path, association, dissociation, presence, absence, separation, non-disappearance.

The *Paṭṭhāna* generally concentrates on the plurality of causes rather than a single cause that brings about an effect. For example, a seed growing into a plant. First of all the seed must be good enough to plant, there must be soil and water, if not the plant will not grow. Hence these conditions can have different relations to the effect; the *Paṭṭhāna* works out twenty-four such relations mentioned above. In the *Paṭṭhāna-Nāya,* a plurality of conditions that help shape an event are microscopically considered. There is the conditioning state and the conditioned state. In this system of teaching, causation is a calculus of possibilities, energies, and is applied to the problem of liberation by way of an analyses of the relations of mental and physical states. In other words, "this means that when a state is present, the others connected with it will either arise, if they have not arisen, continue to exist, if they already exist, or gradually develop, while existing."[1] The belief in the efficacy of *bhāvanā* (mental cultivation), involves a programmatic progression, i.e., the association with certain wholesome states and dissociation from others.

It might be questioned whether this relatedness is objectively given as a feature of the world or, a product of the mind. Objectivity is only a relative notion. Subject and object arise together or not at all. This view is somewhat parallel to William James' theory of relation in western philosophy. He rejects one-sidedness of both realism and subjective idealism in their attempt to bifurcate experience into discrete categories of inner and outer, subject and object.[2]

Relations are neither constructions of the mind nor objectively given but part of a felt unity. Buddhism proceeds along similar line but from a profoundly meditative perspective. *Kamma* is one of the twelve links which constitute the wheel of life and death taught by the Buddha in another book of the *Abhidhamma Piṭaka* called *Vibhaṅga*. To sum up, we can see that Buddha's teachings consist of three aspects:

doctrinal, practical, and realizable. That is, whatever arises or ceases does so due to an interplay of a plurality of causes. Nothing can exist by itself alone: when the conditions that support a thing's existence cease, so does the thing itself.

The principle of conditionality lies at the heart of the Buddha's enlightenment. Conditionality is often used as a synonym for causality. That is, whatever arises or ceases does so due to an interplay of a plurality of causes. Nothing can exist alone by itself. When the conditions that support a thing's existence cease, so does the thing itself. In Buddhism, things have been in motion since the beginningless beginning. This motion, or dynamism, is known in Buddhism as *anicca*—change, impermanence—it is one of the characteristics of existence. Insubstantiality (*anattā*) and dissatisfaction (*dukkha*) are the two other characteristics. Thus, these are the three marks of existence.

In its analysis of energy (*satti*), Buddhism goes beyond the boundaries of conventional modern science. The latter recognizes only four fundamental forces of nature, that is, electromagnetic (between electric charges), nuclear (between protons and neutrons), gravitational (between masses including the universal force of inertia), and weak (between any kind of particles). In Buddhism, the mind is also a force. It is the energetic exercise of the disciplined mind on matter that serves our goal, the *nibbāna*. Dependent origination is a universal law applicable to both mental and physical forces. Life is a phenomena rooted in psychic processes that successively proceed one after the other in a cause-effect relationship. The Buddha categorized these processes in a special formula called dependent origination (*paticcasamuppāda*). It is translated as causal conditioning or causal genesis. The whole causal formula called dependent origination consists of 12 interdependent causes and effects, technically called conditions (*paccaya*). It seems that things are conditional. Nothing is independent or isolated. Dependent origination is an unbroken process. In this process, nothing is stable or fixed. In Buddhism life is not opposed to death. The basic unity of life-death is expressed in the notion of co-relativity. This is implicit in the Four Noble Truths such as suffering, the origin of suffering, the cessation of suffering, and the path leading to the cessation of suffering, or the Noble Eightfold Path.

This doctrine is a discourse on the process of birth and death and not a philosophical theory of the evolution of the world. It deals with the cause of rebirth and suffering with a view to helping man get rid of the ills of life. It does not talk about the riddle or mystery of life. It merely explains the simple arising of a state—dependent on its antecedent state. In Buddhist countries there is a general belief that life is not worthy enough if one does not try to understand the Four Noble

Truths, the law of kamma, and the doctrine of *paticcasamuppāda*. Also Very Venerable Taungpulu Sayadaw tried his best to teach everyone who visited him, especially the law of *kamma* or law of causation. It is due to ignorance (*avijjā*)—which is deep delusion—that we are circling round, says the Buddha. When the ignorance is destroyed and turned into insight, all causality is shattered as in the case of the Enlightened Ones. Those who have destroyed delusion and broken through the dense darkness will wander no more.

Turning now to the *Paṭṭhāna,* the book of causal relations, it has been said, "This is the most important and most voluminous book of the *Abhidhamma Piṭaka*. One who patiently reads this treatise cannot but admire the profound wisdom and penetrative insight of the Buddha."[3] The term *paṭṭhāna* is composed of the prefix "pa" various and "thana" relation or condition *(paccaya).* It is so called because it deals with the 24 modes of causal relations which will be explained in depth later on. The importance attached to this treatise is revealed in its nick-name: *mahā-pakaraṇa*—the Great Book:

> And while he contemplated the content of the Dhammasangani, his body did not emit rays. And similarly, with the contemplation of the next five books, but when coming to the Great Book, he began to contemplate the twenty-four universal causal relations of condition, of presentation, and so on, His omniscience certainly found its opportunity therein.[4]

These 24 Co-relations are very important, but the importance does not lie in the number of modes, but in the concept of modal occurrence. It provides an explanation of all existents not only in their spatial and temporal relations but as factors in the process of liberation. It also serves to indicate that causation is much more complicated than simple temporal succession. Antecedents (*purejāta*) and post occurrence (*pacchajāta*) are only two modes of relating. Whatever exists can be analyzed in terms of this co-relationality. *Paṭṭhāna* is the teaching of *anattā*. In the *Anattā Sutta* the Buddha expounded in "Body, monks, is not self." But he also expounded, "Oneself is the guardian of oneself. What other guardian would there be? With oneself fully controlled, one obtains a refuge which is hard to gain."[5]

The question of whether "I" exist, and whether "you" exist now comes into focus. This question was brought to the Buddha, and today we are still asking it. According to *Abhidhamma*, "I am real," and "you are real." We exist. But we exist not in the way we see ourselves and each other. What we see is an image of what we think we see or would like to see. Therefore, we can say there are more than one I, and more than two you 's. The "I" of the senses, and the subtle "I," and this subtle "I" is the real "I"—the psycho-physical phenomena or the Five Aggregates. When we see just the "I" of the senses we give different names: man, woman, animals, etc. As we go one practicing, then a day will come when we will be able to see the real "I" and the conventional appearance will disappear. When we have our understanding, we will be able to differentiate the real from the unreal, and truth from imagination. Very Venerable Taungpulu Sayadaw helped clarify the Buddha's teaching by saying that when two individuals meet they become six individuals. He says the three I's are: the "I" that you see, the "I" that I feel I am, and the real "I." There are also three "you's."

This conditional relation is the teaching of insubstantiality *(anattā)* which is a difficult doctrine to grasp. It is really difficult to think about ourselves as insubstantial when what happens in our lives seems so real. Since the grip on the "I" is so strong, without practice experiential knowledge of *anattā,* one of the three marks of existence, cannot arise.

The other two marks of existence are *anicca* (impermanence), and *dukkha* (dissatisfactoriness). Impermanence is concealed by continuity. Take candlelight for example. When one looks at the flame of the candle, one may think it is the same flame. In reality, the flame is constantly appearing and disappearing from moment to moment, but we are disillusioned by one single same flame because of the idea and of continuity. With regards to dissatisfactoriness, it is our nature to turn away from suffering, thus, *dukkha* is concealed by movement.

In essence, *paṭṭhāna* conceives and speaks about reality as different kinds of conditions which arise and pass away at every moment without a break. These conditions are responsible for all stages of the animal, plant, and mineral formations in life.

Co-relationality can also be understood from the point of view of "association." It is a descriptive feature of the mind that consciousness and mental factors co-nascently (*sahajāta*) arise, that is, arise together, or not at all. These co-arisen factors are called mind (*citta*) and it is mind that imposes order on the world. Hence, the *Dhammapada* states, "Mind is the forerunner of all phenomena. Mind is the chief, they are mind-made."[6] In dependent origination, the re-linking consciousness (*paṭisandicitta*) gives rise to mind and matter (*nāma-rūpa*). Their relation is one of antecedence (*purejāta*), sufficiency (*upanissaya*) and contiguity (*anantara*). In Buddhism, we are bound to become (*bhava*) not only for what we think but for how we think, i.e., the thinking mechanism.

The last major application of the law of causation to be considered is that of Ethical Reciprocity (*kamma*). Causation, or law of kamma, involves volition which carries ethical import. For instance, all activities which either assist or injure. It states in the *Dhammapada*: "An evil deed that is done does not curdle at once, just like milk. Smoldering, like fire covered by ashes, it follows the fool."[7] Direct insight into the law of cause and effect is said to be the product of advanced meditative practice; it is this insight which opens the path to real freedom.

The 24 Co-relations are separate strands of the same rope. Multifold are the ways in which one thing or one occurrence may be the condition for some other thing or occurrence. In the *Paṭṭhāna,* the 24 modes of conditionality are explained and then applied to all conceivable mental and physical phenomena and occurrences. In this way, their conditioned nature is demonstrated. The 24 modes of conditionality are:

Root Condition (hetu paccaya). The root condition is compared to the root of a tree. Just as a tree rests on its roots and remains above only as long as its root is not destroyed, similarly all kammically wholesome and unwholesome mental states are entirely dependent on the presence of their respective roots, that is, of greed, hatred, delusion (unwholesome roots). or, non-greed, non-hatred, and non-delusion (wholesome roots).

It is called "root" because it functions like the roots of a tree, and "conditioned" because it relates as cause to produce the effect. The roots are firmly fixed to the ground and take up water and nutriments to feed the trunk and branches; the root prevents the tree from falling down when it is blown about by winds or pushed against. As long as the roots are firm and functioning, the trees grow and develop. Just as the roots are related to the trees as the basis for existence, growth, development and stabilizing, so also good and bad actions performed by beings in the world are like trees. And the six roots—greed, hatred, delusion, non-greed, non-hatred, and non-delusion—are like the roots of a tree. All actions originate from these six roots. These six roots, are the conditioning states. Just as a tree grows and expands with the increase in the size and length of their roots, so also the human population in the unhappy planes of existence increase with the increase of the unwholesome roots, and the populations of the happy planes of existence increase with the wholesome roots. Just as the trees die when there are no roots, so also, when the six roots as causes are absent, there is cessation from the round of rebirths.

Object Condition (*ārammanapaccaya*). The condition where a conditioning state as object relates by causing other states to arise is known as object-condition or the relation of object. All classes of consciousness, all kinds of mental factors, all phases of *nibbāna,* all those terms called concepts are object-conditions. There is, in fact, not a single thing which does not become an object of mind and of mental factor. Briefly, there are six kinds of objects: (a) visible objects, (b) audible objects, (c) odorous objects, (d) taste objects, (e) tangible objects, consisting of hardness, heat, and motion, and (f) cognizable objects (mind objects) like different types of consciousness, mental factors, *nibbāna,* and the concepts. All objects are past, present, and future, except *nibbāna* and concepts which are time freed. No time is necessary for them. Consciousness and mental factors form the supports to the corresponding six kinds of consciousness and the mental phenomena associated therewith. For example, just as a weak or old man has to depend on a stick or crutches to get-up or walk, so also, consciousness or mental factors have to depend on the six kinds of objects for their existence. So consciousness and mental factors gather strength from the six kinds of objects.

Predominance Condition (*adhipaṭipaccaya*). Literally, this means mastery or lordship over one's own mind, namely, factors such as wish, thought, effort, and reasoning. By way of analogy, this condition is like a universal monarch who, with regard to influence and authority, has no rival and rules with absolute sovereignty over the four islands. So, if one of the four predominant states is a conditioning state, the remaining three, together with all the associated neutral states have to follow it as a conditioned state. Owing to the existence of these four dominants, there exist distinguished or dignified saintly persons like Christ, Buddha, Mother Mary, Lady of Fatima, etc, Owing to the appearance of such personages, there appears practice of all the dominant states for the general prosperity and welfare of mankind.

Proximity Condition (*anantarapaccaya*) and *Contiguity Condition* (*samanantarapaccaya*). Proximity and Contiguity Conditions are almost identical but there is a slight variation. With regards to contiguity—if the king is not there (has died) his heir will take the place (uninterruptedness). With regards to Proximity—here if the king does not die but becomes a monk, then his son will take the throne and perform the duties (nearness).

Co-Existence Condition (*sahajātapaccaya*). Certain states, things, etc., arise together. When the sun rises, at the same time heat and light arise. Similarly, when we see the four aggregates, the fifth also arises.

Reciprocity or Mutuality Condition (*aññamaññapaccaya*). For example, a tripod has three legs. When it is set up it will be able to stand on account of the interdependence of its three legs, but if one of these legs is broken, the remaining two legs cannot make the tripod stand. It is like the saying, "United we stand, divided we fail."

Dependence Condition (*nissayapaccaya*). The example here is that the tree depends on the soil to provide a medium for the tree to set down its roots, and the brush dipped in paint depends on the canvas to provide a flat surface for the paint to be placed. This condition illustrates dependence by way of needing a base.

Sufficing Condition or Strong Dependence Condition (*upanissayapaccaya*). This condition is like the rain on which trees depend for their growth and beings depend for their well-being. Here the trees and the beings depend greatly on the rain. Let me clarify ordinary dependence and strong dependence. For obtaining cooked rice, first of all there must be rice. So, paddy seeds, a plot of land, and rain are the primary things to produce rice, and this primary dependence is strong dependence. But once rice is obtained, it is only necessary to depend on the cooking pot, fuel, fire, water, and the cook to boil the rice. This is ordinary or sufficing condition.

Pre-existence Condition (*purejātapaccaya*). Literally, that which pre-exists. This condition is like the sun and moon which appear at the beginning of the world, which do not disappear and which provide light, heat to the people who come after.

Past-existence Condition (*pacchajātapaccaya*). For example, the rain water that falls every subsequent year renders service by way of past existence to such vegetation as has grown up in previous years in promoting its growth and development.

Repetition Condition (*āsevanapaccaya*). For example, if you save money since childhood you become well-off when you grow old, because you have done the same thing repeatedly. All the great and wonderful discoveries, supernormal powers, attainment of path and fruit, and the practice of the perfections to become higher beings are not possible without repetition condition.

Kamma Condition (*kammapaccaya*). "As ye sow, so shall ye reap." This condition is like the chief disciple or the chief carpenter who encourages himself to make efforts to complete his own task and encourages the assistants, the younger carpenters to complete their individual tasks wlth their efforts. Beings are born of this condition. It is called kamma because of a peculiar function which is volition or will itself, and it dominates every action. Kamma is that which creates through the use of thought, words, and action.

Effect or Resultant Condition (*vipākapaccaya*). The examples to explain this condition are the fruits which have ripened and flowers which have bloomed. This condition brings attention to the change of state from infancy or youth to maturity.

Nutriment Condition (*āhārapaccaya*). This condition is like the pillar which supports an old house to prevent it from falling down and being destroyed. We have physical nutriment and mental nutriment. Physical nutriment is the support which when ingested enables the body's activities to be carried out. Mental nutriments are contact, volition, and consciousness.

Control or Faculty Condition (*indriyapaccaya*). Like four countries —each one located in one of the four directions—which govern themselves. By not interfering with their neighbors, all enjoy the freedom of control in their own sphere.

Absorption Condition (*jhānapaccaya*). Absorption means to look at closely or to view actively. That is, going close to the object and looking at it mentally. This condition is like holding the arrow firmly and directing the aim. The meditator directs the mind towards the object and keeps it steadfastly in view in order to have a clear understanding of its meaning. Absorption or *jhāna* consists of five progressive steps: (a) *vitakka* (directing the mind toward the object and fixing it firmly; (b) *vicāra,* sustaining the mind on the object to get the better view; (c) *pīti,* creating interest in the object. This makes the mind happy and content; (d) *uppekhā,* equanimity, once the mind is established firmly it gets balance; (e) *ekaggatā,* one pointed concentration.

Path Condition (*maggapaccaya*). There are various paths; if one takes a wrong path, one suffers. If one takes the right path, it leads to happiness, and even to *nibbāna.* The difference between *jhāna* and magga conditions are *jhāna* condition fixes the mind directly and firmly on the object. *Magga* condition fixes the volition directly on the path. Path condition is responsible for our birth and re-birth.

Association Condition (*sampayuttapaccaya*). This condition is like a cup of tea which consists of (a) tea leaves, (b) sugar, (c) cream, and (d) hot water. When all of the ingredients are thoroughly mixed together, the taste cannot be distinguished as that of tea, sugar, water, and milk separately.

Dissociation Condition (*vippayuttapaccaya*). This condition is like a mixture of six flavors: sweet, sour, hot, salty, astringent, and bitter. Although they are together, they remain separate. The sweet does not become sour, and vice-versa. Another example is that we cannot mix water and mercury or oil and water. They remain separate, even when we shake them. The condition makes it easy to identify the parts.

Presence Condition (*atthipaccaya*). Because of the big mountain's shade, the trees grow well. Because of the presence of a developed being, we can feel strong inspiration. The presence condition has two forces. One is production, and the other is support. The big mountains support the trees, herbs, flowers, etc. So also, earth supports and produces those green fresh trees with their nutritive power.

Absence Condition (*natthipaccaya*). The absence condition can be illustrated by thinking of a woodburning fire. If there is no wood to be found, if the wood is absent, there can be no fire.

Disappearance Condition (*vigatapaccaya*). Disappearance condition is similar to absence condition but the time element is involved. With the gradual setting of the sun, the night arises. If a person leaves your company, you can still visualize them.

Non-Disappearance Condition (*avigatapaccaya*). Non-disappearance condition is like presence condition which supports and produces. For example, water is the condition for the fish to live comfortably. As long as the water does not disappear, the fish will be there, too.

Remember the meaning of *paṭṭhāna*. It means the pre-eminent or principle cause. Every act has a cause. There are two kinds of effect: the direct and the indirect.

> By the direct effect is meant the primary or actual effect; by "the indirect" is meant the consequent or incidental effect. Of these two kinds, only the direct effect is here referred to as ineluctable, and for this reason—that it never fails to arise when its proper cause is established or brought into play. And the indirect effect is to be understood as 'eluctable' since it may or may not arise even though its cause is fully established. Thus the ineluctable cause is so named with reference to the ineluctable effect. Hence ineluctable or principal cause alone is meant to be expounded in the "Great Treatise." For this reason the name '*Paṭṭhāna*' is assigned to the entire collection of the twenty-four relations, and also to the "Great Treatise."
>
> And now, to make the matter more clear and simple.
>
> Say that greed springs into being within a man who desires to get money and grain. Under the influence of greed, he goes to a forest where he clears a piece of land and establishes fields, yards and gardens, and starts to work very hard. Eventually he obtains plenty of money and grain by reason of his gains, looks after his family, and performs many virtuous deeds, from which also he will reap rewards in his future existences. In this illustration, all the mental and material states coexisting with greed, are called direct effects. Apart from these, all the outcomes, results and rewards, which are to be enjoyed later on in his future existences, are called indirect effects. Of these two kinds of effects, only the former is dealt with in the *Paṭṭhāna*. However, the latter kind finds its place in the Suttanta discourses. If this exists, then that happens; or, because of the occurrence of this, that also takes place: such an exposition is called "expounding by way of Suttanta." In fact, the three states (greed, hate, and ignorance are called the hetus or

> conditions, because they are the roots whence spring the defilements of the whole animate world, of the whole inanimate world, and of the world of space. The three other opposite states (disinterestedness, amity, and knowledge) are also called hetus or conditions, since they are the roots whence springs purification. In the same manner the remainder of the *Paṭṭhāna* relations are to be understood in their various senses. Thus must we understand that all things that happen, occur, take place, or produce changes, are solely the direct and indirect effects, results, outcomes, or products of these twenty-four *Paṭṭhāna* relations or causes.[8]

If you find difficulty remembering all 24 Co-relations remember that they can be condensed into four conditions:

Object Condition (*arammanapaccaya*). There is not a single thing which does not become an object of attention. For example, visible objects, audible objects, etc. Mind is always running towards an object.

Sufficient Condition (*upanissayapaccaya*). Due to sufficient condition all that has been seen, heard, smelled, tasted, touched, and experienced in days, months, years long gone by takes form again at the mind door, even after a lapse of thirty to fifty years, if sufficient cause is available. And so people remember their past and can utter such expressions as "I experienced it before," "I heard it a long time ago," and so on. Another example would be that in order to grow healthy trees, the trees depend greatly on rain and soil. Cold is related to solidification of water; heat is related to the melting of wax, iron, and gold. Good medicine is related to the physical well-being of sick and diseased people.

Kamma or Action Condition (*kammapaccaya*). Volition dominates every action. Volition is predominant in all actions. *Kamma* is that by which creatures act, think, and talk. All the actions of beings are determined by this volition. We all have this condition. The happiness and unhappiness experienced by beings are the result of this action.

Presence Condition (*atthipaccaya*). It is the relation of presence causally relating itself to its effect by being present along with the effect. By this condition there are forces of presence and also presence of support. The presence of the group of mental states which takes the words, "one's own," or "my" which is a wrong view. The right view is mentality-materiality. "Presence" here means "presence" after having arisen. Therefore, *nibbāna* is not included in the Presence Condition. Once you attain *nibbāna*, you go beyond conditioned to the unconditioned state. This is the end of the ways of the 24 Co-relations.

5

Clarification of the Buddha's Psycho-Ethical Attitude

Before investigating the subject of the Buddha's psycho-ethical attitude, it is important first of all to introduce Buddhism in a minimally controversial form. Scholars and commentators have written and continue to write books on all aspects of Buddhism; consequently there is a wealth of literature. According to J.B. Pratt:

> The oldest books that tell of the Buddha's life and teaching were not put completely into writing until about the year 30 B.C. Doubtless they go back in the oral memory of the Buddhistic community very much farther than this; and some of the materials from which they were formed may have been derived from the immediate disciples of the founder, some may have come from his very lips.[1]

Based on such foundations, Pali scholars have worked out the most trustworthy texts, known as the *Tipiṭaka*, which I have already mentioned in the earlier chapters. Gratitude can never be fully expressed for their tremendous expositions, on which the scholars of Buddhism have to depend for their references. Even so, the opinions of different readers will vary.

Before going further, this writer would like to say a few words about the most common of the many names used by Buddhists to designate the founder of their religion. The term "Buddha" is not a proper name but a title, as is the word "Christ." As Christ means the Anointed One, so Buddha means the Enlightened One, or the One

Fully Awake. According to Buddhistic theory, there has been a long line of Buddhas. The family name of the one we know was Gotama (in Sanskrit, *Gautama*), and his personal name was Siddhattha (Sanskrit: *Sidhartha*), which means "wish-fulfilling," or "one whose purpose has been achieved." He came from the clan of the Śākyas, and hence came to be known in later years as Śākyamuni, or the sage of the Śākyas. His disciples, both those who briefly knew him and those who had been his followers for years, frequently referred to him as the Blessed One. Perhaps the most common title found in the Pali books is "Tathāgata," which has no exact English equivalent but which means approximately "one who has thus-come and thus-gone," a perfect one.

From the study of the Nikāyas, perhaps the most striking feature about Buddha is his unique combination of a scientific mind and sympathetic heart. His pity for every sort of sentient life and his devotion to their needs seems to have been boundless. Yet he never lost his head, and was never misled or blinded by sentiments.

> I think that Rhys Davids and Oldenberg and Neumann are in part right in picturing the Buddha as a rationalistic moralist; but Keith and Franke and La Vallee Poussin are also right in pointing out that there were other sides to his character and teaching. He made repeated use, as we shall see, of methods of meditation borrowed from the Yogins of his time and taught them to his disciples; and he took for granted (often in somewhat amused fashion, to be sure) the gods of Indian tradition.[2]

There is no reason to suspect that the Buddha denied the existence of God. But one thing is definite and clear: he refused to discuss such ultimate problems, like God, soul, world, and so on. The great mass of the Buddha's dialogues are concerned with moral and humanistic matters. The Buddha was primarily a moral teacher. It was on the question of right living that he placed supreme emphasis, and upon the psychological analysis and the spiritual training which he considered helpful or necessary for attaining the ideals of human life.

Buddhism is a doctrine of salvation or a path of deliverance (*vimutti-magga*) for it is in the problem of *dukkha*, suffering, and its complete elimination that Buddhism is mainly interested. As Piyadassi Thera states:

> The Buddha is such a seer, and his path to deliverance is open to all who have eyes to see and minds to understand...The Buddha's foremost admonition to his...disciples was that the Dhamma should

be promulgated for the welfare and happiness of many; out of compassion for the world.[3]

As a man he attained Buddhahood and proclaimed to the world the latent inconceivable possibilities and the creative power of man. Instead of placing an unseen almighty God over human beings, one who arbitrarily controls their destinies, and making them subservient to a supreme power, he raised the work of the individual to a crucial level: one where each person, through effort and energy, can gain deliverance and purification without depending on an external god or mediating priests. It was Buddha who taught the egocentric world the noble ideal of selfless service. It was he who exposed the degrading caste system, taught equality of all people, and brought attention to the dignity of the individual.

There are a number of doctrines through which the Buddha's analysis of human existence can be understood. There is the twelve-fold chain, or circle of causes and effects—the theory of conditioned origination (*paṭiccasamuppāda*). According to this teaching, all phenomena, all beings and things, are effects which result from a complex of causes; they are dependent in their origination upon that combination of causes and have no identity apart from them. Buddha attached so much importance to the understanding of this insight that he called it *Dhamma,* truth.

> Let us put aside questions of the Beginning and the End...I will teach you the *Dhamma*: That being thus, this comes to be. From the coming to be of that, this arises. That being absent, this does not happen. From the cessation of that, this ceases. He who sees the *Paticcasamuppada* sees the *Dhamma*, and he who sees the *Dhamma*, sees the *Paticcasamuppada*.[4]

This theory is very profound, says Buddha.

> Profound, Ananda, is Dependent Origination, and profound of appearance. It is through not understanding this doctrine, Ananda, through no penetrating it, that thus mankind is like an entangled warp, or to an ensnarled web, or to muñja grass and pabbaja-grass, and fails to extricate itself from punishment, suffering, perdition, rebirth.[5]

There is also the presentation of the essentials in the form of the Four Noble Truths: life is marked by suffering, suffering has a cause which is craving, the cause can be made to cease, and it can be made to cease by following a path of eight steps.

Again, there is a well known and frequently used characterization of all life in terms of the three marks of existence: suffering, impermanence and non-substantiality or impersonality. In every case the starting point is *dukkha,* the suffering, pain or grief which is the common lot of all living beings. For the Buddha, this is what constituted the problem to be solved; it was from here that all his thinking started and it was to the curing of this condition that all his effort was directed. As Floyd Ross observes:

> Gautama did not find it easy to keep each seeker in touch with the concrete aspects of the problems. Not all of his associates had an equally keen awareness of the dangers implicit in dealing with a human problem primarily on the level of abstract concepts. This is well illustrated by a story in the Sutta-Nipata. One day a certain teacher came to Gautama to instruct him in purity. True purity, Gautama was told, comes only from philosophy...Inward peace comes neither from philosophy nor from the absence of philosophical opinions. He who holds to a philosophical position is concerned with defending it. This leads to disputation with rival opinions which in turn leads to pride, arrogance, and conceit. Actually, one should get to the place where he neither desires opinions nor their absence. The genuine sage is the man who has shaken all "systems" of philosophy. Having no position to defend, he has no special prejudice to plead.[6]

When a certain person asked the Buddha whether the world is eternal or non-eternal, finite or infinite, he commented:

> The religious life does not depend on the dogma that the world is eternal, nor does the religious life depend on the dogma that the world is not eternal. Whether the dogma obtain that the world is eternal, or that the world is not eternal, there still remain birth, old age, death, sorrow, lamentation, misery, grief and despair, for the extinction of which in the present life I am prescribing.[7]

Metaphysical theorizing is, therefore, a fetter. It does not lead in the direction of supreme wisdom. Hence the Buddha refuses to create a conjectured theory for his questioner.

Another kind of question seems to have occurred rather frequently. Is the person who has achieved deliverance reborn? Such a question was more mundane than questions about the world's finitude or infinity. Apparently, the Upaniṣadic teaching on immortality had not aided the average person who was still talking about deliverance in terms of the popular theories of rebirth and after-lives.

To face such a speculative question while recognizing the honesty of the questioner required patience and skill. The Buddha pointed out that it is not correct to raise the question in that form at all, and used the analogy of fire. A fire burns only so long as there is fuel. The fire becomes extinct when the fuel has been used up. It is pointless to ask where the fire has gone—east, west, north or south. It is equally pointless to ask where the saints have gone. The person who has been released from the ordinary forms and entanglements of sensory life is "... deep, immeasurable, unfathomable, like and mighty ocean. To say that he is reborn would not fit the case. To say that he is both reborn and not reborn would not fit the case. To say that he is neither reborn nor not reborn would not fit the case."[8] In other words, true joy cannot be verbalized. Cessation of craving is something that can only be experienced from within. In Theravada Buddhist tradition, "the final step in the attainment of Arahatship occurs when the *āsavas* (defilements) are destroyed."[9] It is this extinction of the defilements, initially rooted in *tanhā* (thirst) which is viewed as the true liberation of *nibbāna*.

This is the Buddha's doctrine of hope, an affirmation that we can do something about our predicament. Moreover Buddha is convinced by his own experience that the highest reality dwells within us. This reality is within the individual but beyond the individual; one must, therefore, first overcome the individual limitations of consciousness if one wants to attain it, otherwise it will be like "a man who has found the elixir of immortality and who has no vessel wherein to keep it."[10] Buddha considered suffering to be the common and all-pervasive experience of humankind, and he sought ways to resolve the problems it poses. The Buddha's teachings are more deeply and directly concerned with truth and the pragmatic importance of things, more with what Dr. Malalasekera calls "spiritual health," than with theories.[11]

It must always be born in mind that Buddhism is primarily a way of life and, therefore, it is with the human personality that it is almost wholly concerned. The Buddha claimed that this was a practical teaching; its object was to show a way of escape from the ever-revolving round of birth-and-death, which constitutes *saṁsāra* and which is considered a condition of degradation and suffering (*dukkha*). Constantly the Buddha came back to the point that there is nothing wrong with life or death but with the attitude that people hold toward them. People try to possess life and cling to it. But everything is conditioned and relative, including the five *khandhas* which constitute the totality of each person, hence there is really nothing to which to cling. There is neither person nor any lasting entity. The person who ignores the principles of unrest in things—the intrinsic nature of suffering—is upset when confronted with the vicissitudes of life, because he has not trained his mind to see things as they really are.

Our clinging to pleasures leads to much vexation when things occur contrary to our expectations. It is therefore necessary to cultivate a detached outlook towards life and things pertaining to life. Detachment cannot bring about frustration, disappointment and mental torment, because there is no clinging to one thing or another, but instead, a letting go. Indeed this is not easy, but it is the sure remedy for controlling, if not eradicating, unsatisfactoriness. The Buddha sees suffering as suffering, and happiness as happiness, and explains that all cosmic pleasure, like all other conditioned things, is evanescent, a passing show. It is hard indeed to be undisturbed when touched by the sufferings of life, but the man who cultivates equanimity is not upset.

A mother was asked why she did not lament over the death of her beloved son. Her answer was philosophical: "Uninvited he came, uninvited he passed away, as he came so he went, what use is there in lamenting, weeping and wailing?"[12] In such a manner may people bear their misfortune, with equanimity; such is the advantage of a tranquil mind. It is unshaken by loss and gain, blame and praise, and undisturbed by adversity.

This frame of mind is brought about by viewing the sentient world in proper perspective. Thus, calmness or evenness of mind leads to enlightenment and deliverance from suffering. This pragmatic approach of the Buddha leads people onto the path of *Dhamma,* where is no use for superstition, speculation, or musing. His method is that of psychological analysis, and he contributed to the spiritual growth of humanity through an honest and unbiased expression of his thought and experience. The goal of his message was deliverance, not to form or reform any religion. He was a pure scientific thinker who wanted to understand and interpret the natural phenomena rationally, without any religious or non-religious interferences. But the Buddha was also a practical man. Modern pragmatists William James and John Dewey would totally agree with the Buddha's principles of practicality. His practicality was his experience of the Truth and not mere knowledge of it. This is the foundation of Buddhism. Gotama Buddha wanted everybody to tread on his path in order to become enlightened. The Buddha says in the *Dhammapada*: "A well-bred person [a Buddha] is difficult to be found. He is not born anywhere. Wherever such a wise man is born that household prospers."[13]

The facts mentioned above clearly explain that the Buddha was not a savior in the theological sense, nor was he any ordinary person. He was a *mahāpurisa* (lit., Great Being). Hence his physical form became the object of worship within the Theravada Buddhist world. Monywe Sayadaw of Burma and others, for example, recommended the worship of the thirty-two marks of the Great Being. According to U Pe Maung Tin, "the superhuman marks are the results of good deeds done in former births and can only be maintained in the present life by righteousness." He continues, saying that the Buddha called a man of the following four qualities very wise, a superman:

> (1) He concerns himself with the advantages and the happiness of the common people. He has established many of them in the noble system, that is, in the beauty of righteousness set forth in the Noble Path. (2) He can think about a thing, or not, just as he pleases; for he has control over his mind in the trends of thought. (3) He can enter without toil or trouble into the four stages of ecstatic meditation that are beyond thought, and yet pertain to this present life, (4) He has thus put away the cankers arising from lust, and attains and realizes a same emancipation of heart and mind even in this present life. This discourse goes on to say that the Buddha himself has done all this.[14]

The Buddha encouraged his disciples not to be morbid, but to cultivate the all important quality of joy (*piti*), which is one of the Factors of Enlightenment. The result of this admonition of the Buddha is seen in the *Psalms of the Early Buddhists*,[15] in which are recorded the joyful songs (*udāna*) of his disciples, male and female. A dispassionate study of Buddhism will tell us that it is a message radiating joy and hope. The Buddha says in the *Dhammapada*: "Let us live happily, then, we who possess nothing. Let us dwell feeding on happiness like the shining gods."[16] From this it can be clearly seen that Buddhism is not a defeatist philosophy of pessimism. Today in the scientific world there are diverse attempts to improve the conditions of the world. Many improvements and advantages have resulted, but all of them are based on the material and the external. Scientists and technologists try to improve the world, try to control the environment, try to make the world comfortable. But according to the ideas of Buddhism, such as the doctrine of the impermanence of all things (*anicca*), external manipulations alone cannot make the world free from sorrow. To get rid of sorrow, one must understand the world within, one must develop the inner faculties of one's own mind. The Buddha said: "Mind your own mind!"[17] "The wise tame themselves."[18]

To understand the world within, it is necessary to have guidance, the instruction of a competent and genuine seer whose clarity of vision and depth of insight penetrate into the deepest recesses of life. Humanity is caught in a tangle, inner as well as outer, and the Buddha's infallible remedy, in brief, is this: "The prudent man full of Effort, well established in Virtue, develops Concentration and Wisdom and succeeds in solving the tangle."[19]

The whole dispensation of the master is permeated with the boundless quality of universal love (*metta*). *Sīla,* or virtue, the initial stage of the Path, is based on this loving compassion, and loving kindness. To abstain from evil and to do good is the function of *sīla*, the code of conduct taught in Buddhism.[20] *Sīla* embraces love, modesty, tolerance, pity, charity and happiness at the success of others. *Samādhi* and *pañña,* or concentration and wisdom, are concerned with the discipline of the mind. In Buddhist ethics, it is clear that the code of conduct set forth by the Buddha is a career paved with good intentions for the welfare and happiness of all beings everywhere. Buddhist moral principles aim at making society secure by promoting unity, harmony and right relations among people. In the Buddhist code of conduct, *sīla* is the first stepping stone of the Buddhist way of life. It is the basis for mental development. *Sīla* or virtue nourishes mental life and makes it steady and calm.

The next step in the path to deliverance is mental culture (*bhāvanā*) and concentration (*samādhi*). The correct practice of *samādhi* maintains the mind and the mental properties in a state of balance. Through mastery of the mind, by not allowing the mind to master him, the yogi cultivates true wisdom (*pañña*). True wisdom means insight or right understanding of life as it really is. A man of right understanding is immune to all impurities.

These three principles, virtue, concentration and wisdom, function together for one common end: deliverance of the mind (*ceto-vimutti*). It is through genuine cultivation of one's mind, and through control of actions both physical and verbal, that purity is attained. It is now clear that to tread the Noble Eightfold Path (*ariya atthaṅgika magga*), which is arranged in three groups—virtue, concentration and wisdom—one needs to cultivate the highest purification, perfect mental health free from all tainted impulses. One cannot function independently of the others. These three go together supporting each other. Virtue, or regulated behavior, strengthens meditations and meditation in turn promotes wisdom. Wisdom helps one to see life as it really is, that is, to see life and all things pertaining to life as arising and passing away. As it is found in the *Dīgha Nikāya*: "As hand washes hand, and foot washes foot, so does conduct purify wisdom and wisdom conduct."[21] This fact may be born in mind by students of Buddhism, especially in the academic circles, so that the teachings of the Buddha may be seen not as mere speculation or a doctrine of metaphysics devoid of practical value or importance.

The Buddha used strong language to warn his followers against mere book learning. Concerning an aspirant's endeavors, the Buddha admonishes:

> Even if he recites a large number of scriptural texts but, being slothful, does not act accordingly, he is like a cowherd counting the cows of others, he has no share in religious life.
>
> Even if he recites only a small number, if he is one who acts tightly in accordance with the law, he having forsaken passion, hatred and folly, being possessed of true knowledge and serenity of mind, being free of worldly desires both in this world and the next, has a share in the religious life.[22]

The Buddha was not satisfied with any theoretical mode or code of discipline besides one's own intense practice. The Buddha's way of life is a cleansing of one's speech, action and thought. He repudiated what is nowadays called metaphysics, for instance, problems regarding a first cause, or about the ultimate nature and origin of the world. He did not, however, argue his objections to these problems on the ground that they are meaningless—as the modern logical positivist does—but rather on the agnostic ground that no one will ever find the answers, and on the pragmatic ground that even if answers were found, such knowledge would be useless for the sole end which Buddhism sets out to reach, namely, the elimination of all sorrow and suffering.

The Noble Eightfold Path of the Buddha is the best psychophysical method for human perfection. It is by advancing step by step along the ancient path that one reaches the goal: freedom. One cannot attain freedom all at once. As Piyadassi Thera says, "As the sea deepens gradually, so in the doctrine and discipline of the Buddha there is gradual training, gradual doing and gradual practice."[23]

The Buddha's thorough-going treatment is guaranteed to eradicate the cause of the sickly spell and dream of ignorance. No philosophical explanation of man or the universe is required, only this spiritual physician's program of the "psycho-dietetics."[24] A life of strict morality is recommended by Buddha. He is not in favor of codes and conventions, rites and ceremonies.

> There is a story of how Buddha retorted when a Brahmin spoke to him about the virtues attendant on a bath in the river Bahuka. He said that no bath would purify the fool of his sin, even though he bathed as many times as he would wish. The doer of evil, the man of malice, and the perpetrator of crime is never absolved of his sin by baths. One must have his bath in good character.[25]

In Dr. Anil Sarkar's words: "Buddha is fully conscious of the meditative tradition of the Upanishads, but still he differs from the remnant of theoretic element in the Upanishads."[26] The realization of self is a primary step in the Upaniṣads. It is a lengthy process of transcendent experience. Buddhism prescribes rules of disciplines for realizing the final experience of *nibbāna* or liberation. These triadic principles—*sīla*, *samādhi* and *pañña* are not theoretical principles but practical ways for realizing the goal, which is a dispassionate condition, a freedom from the wheel of existence (*bhava cakka*), or in Dr. Sarkar's words: "Freedom from (i) passion and (ii) theoretic propensity and (iii) the life-death-rebirth process."[27] It appears, therefore, that although the ultimate goal is the same in both the Upaniṣadic conception (of which the Buddha was quite aware) and the Buddhistic view, the Buddha's way is completely practical, whereas in the Upaniṣads a theoretical element is involved.

The Buddha outlined the Noble Eightfold Path as a way to attain lasting peace and harmony. The eight parts are: (1) Right Understanding (*sammā diṭṭhi*), and (2) Right Thought (*sammā saṅkappa*), these two being matters of wisdom, they come under *pañña,* the wisdom group; (3) Right Speech (*sammā vācā*), (4) Right Action (*sammā kammānta*), and (5) Right Livelihood (*sammā ājīva*), these three being matters or ethical conduct, they fall under *sīla,* the virtue group; and (6) Right Effort (*sammā vāyāma*), (7) Right Mindfulness (*sammā sati*), and (8) Right Concentration (*sammā samādhi*), these last three being matters of mental development, they come under *samādhi*, the concentration group. These eight factors of the path are arranged according to the *Majjhima Nikāya.*[28] They are not successive stages to be perfected one after another; rather they go hand in hand as aspects of an all-encompassing process.

In this chapter, I have tried to clarify Buddha's psycho-ethical attitude. Ethical disciplines and psychological insights are like the raft by means of which one crosses a river. They are means to an end which cannot be described in terms of the steps one takes in approaching that end. As Chatterjee and Datta observe in *An Introduction to Indian Philosophy:*

> In summing up his teachings, Buddha himself once said: 'Both in the past and even now do I set for just this: suffering (dukkha) and cessation of suffering.' Rhys Davids, quoting this authority observes that the theory of dependent-origination (in its double aspect of explaining the world and explaining the origin of suffering), together with the formula of the Eightfold Path, gives us not only the whole of early Buddhism in a nutshell, but also just those points concerning which we find the most emphatic affirmations of Dhamma as Dhamma ascribed to Gautama.[29]

6

The Process of Thought in Early Buddhist Schools

The Buddha was acknowledged in the early Buddhist Tradition as a *samaṇa*. The nearest equivalent of this in modern English is, perhaps, "philosopher," though this is not altogether satisfactory. The basic meaning of the word *samaṇa* is "one who strives, or labors hard." The earliest generation of Buddhists did not regard the Buddha as a super-human figure of any kind. He had no religious role, such as that of the chosen revealer of divine truth, nor was he regarded by the early Buddhists as a super-human savior in any sense.

The Buddha exhorts his followers to depend on themselves for their deliverance, since both defilement and purity, their presence and absence, and even the degree to which they are present, depend on oneself. One cannot directly purify or defile another. Clarifying his relationship with his followers and emphasizing the importance of self-reliance and individual striving, the Buddha plainly states: you yourself should make the exertion. The Tathagatas are only teachers. As the *Dhammapada* states: "You yourself must strive. The Blessed Ones are (only) preachers. Those who enter the path and practice meditation are released from the Bondage of Mara (death)."[1]

The Buddhas are not redeemers, messiahs, saviors, incarnations, or *avatārs*. Primarily they are teachers who have discovered a great truth which, out of great thier compassion for all beings, they decide to teach. The teaching puts the responsibility on the student to live by the lessons such as those in the *Dhammapada*: "Going on this path, you will end your suffering. This path was preached by me when I became aware of the removal of the thorns (in the flesh)."[2]

The same teaching is repeated in a conversation with Ananda, shortly before the final passing away of the master. The Venerable Ananda, the personal attendant of the Buddha, had been found weeping, and the Buddha, knowing of it, called for him and after comforting him said:

> O Ananda, be ye lamps unto yourselves. Be ye refuge to yourselves. Betake yourselves to no external refuge. Hold fast to the truth as a lamp. Hold fast as a refuge to the truth...And how, Ananda, is a brother to be a lamp unto himself, a refuge unto himself, betaking himself to no external refuge, holding fast to the truth...Looking not for refuge to any one besides himself?[3]

This verse pinpoints that the Buddha has fulfilled all the duties of a real teacher. There is nothing that he has left esoteric. Again and again he kept advising all his disciples to lead a holy life to put an end to all kinds of suffering.

Another distinctive feature of early Buddhist ethics is its freedom from theism; this leaves ample room for rationalism. In G.S.P. Misra's words: "By rejecting animism and ritualism and emphasizing a rational outlook which treats reality as a causally and functionally determined system of plural synergies (*saṃskāras*), the emergence of Buddhism marks an important event in the history of Indian thought."[4] The Buddha insisted that all propositions must be tested, including his own. The testing of these has to take the form of actually living out a disciplined life of morality, meditation and the systematic cultivation of insight.

One of the most important characteristics of the Buddha's teaching, therefore, is the attitude of non-acceptance of traditional orthodoxy of any kind. This differentiates Buddhism from the orthodox theistic religion of the Brahmans of his day. But it does not, of course, differentiate Buddhism from the teachings of other *samaṇas* who, like the Buddha, also rejected traditional orthodoxy. What most clearly differentiated the Buddha's teaching from theirs was his theory of the absolute impermanence of all things (*anicca*) and, above all, his denial of permanent individuality (*anattā*). It is possible, even from what has been discovered so far in the course of this investigation, to see that the Buddha was not hostile to the religious ideas and practices of the ordinary people. He did not endorse these ideas and practices, but neither did he, in general, oppose them.

Buddhism believes in the possibility of self-purification, but only through self-culture, self-discipline, and self-realization; no external rites will help one to achieve inner purity. The spirit of Buddhism is shown in the story narrated in the *Therigātha,* one of the books in the *Tipiṭaka.* It is a discussion between a nun and a Brahman concerning bathing in the river on a cold winter night. The nun said:

> If you could go to heaven by bathing in the river, then surely the fish, tortoises, frogs, water snakes, and crocodiles too will attain heaven. Moreover, if the sins are washed off by bathing, the merits too will be washed off by water...O Brahman, if you are afraid of sins, it is better not to commit them at all.[5]

Again it should not be thought that Buddha had a disrespect for the Vedas; he referred to the Vedas and the Hindu sages with due honor in the course of his sermons to Brahman scholars on several occasions. The Vedic sages and the early Buddhist saints had much in common in their practice of yoga. The Buddha emphasized the need for the deep realization of the sage through meditation, and called upon his disciples to follow the path of renunciation and meditative discipline. Many Buddhist saints acquired supernatural powers through such discipline. The Buddha also taught that all existence is subject to the law of *kamma,* that rebirth is the lot of man, and that suffering is due to attachment—beliefs which were commonly held during his time by followers of the Vedas.

The philosophical basis of early Buddhism is still a subject of controversy. It has been interpreted in many ways, ranging from naive realism to out and out idealism, from absolute monism to radical pluralism. The reason for this is that early Buddhism is sometimes approached from the basis of a subsequent school of Buddhist thought, such as the Sarvāstivāda, or the Mādhyamika. This approach is not historically correct, because it overlooks the historical process at work. Secondly, because it is within the Pali Canon itself, we find statements which lend themselves to different interpretations. In fact it is no exaggeration to say that early Buddhism contains within itself the germs and tendencies of all the schools of Buddhist thought which sprang up centuries later.

In order to work out a way of deliverance it is necessary that one should know the true nature of one's present existence. For it is only when this knowledge is attained that suffering comes to an end. It is with this practical end in view that Buddhism tries to explain the empirical world. It is only within this context that Buddhism as a spiritual discipline becomes clear and meaningful.

The earliest attempt to explain both the individual and the individual in relation to the external world can be seen in three kinds of analyses. The first is the analysis of the individual viewed as the Five Aggregates. The second is the analysis in twelve bases, that is, the sense organs including mind, and their corresponding sense objects. The third is the analysis into eighteen elements, that is, the six sense organs, the six sense objects, and the six kinds of consciousness that arise as a result of the contact between the sense organs and the sense objects.

These three analyses show that there does not exist a soul, a self, a primary substance or a unity. In the final analysis, what is called substance is only compounded dhammas (forces, elements); unity is nothing but a complex of factors. Further, what seems to be one is really many; what is considered permanent is actually in a state of constant change. This is true of mind and matter; both exist as complexes. In the case of living beings, there is no soul which is permanent; and in the case of things, there is no essence which is everlasting. From this Buddhist analysis a basic conclusion can be drawn: that the world is of a plurality of elements. Hence, it is said in the *Majjhima Nikāya*: "The Buddha sees in its true perspective the world which consists of a plurality of elements, a variety of elements."[6]

The basic factors into which the world is arranged are constantly changing. They are arising due to complexes of causes (*paṭicca-samuppāda*). In the *Saṅyutta Nikāya,* physical phenomena (matter) are compared to Mara, the Evil One, or an incurable disease, a festering wound, a piercing arrow, an unbearable pain, a burning fire.[7]

This type of statement is made for the practical purpose of relating how worldly attachments can be cut off. So, also, sometimes the "Five Aggregates into which the individual is analyzed should be considered as void, false, empty, and essenceless."[8] Such characterizations seem to suggest that early Buddhism does not believe in the reality of the empirical world. It is because of such a misinterpretation that Waddell and Kern remarked that early Buddhism is "idealistic nihilism."[9] But a proper understanding of these statements makes such a conclusion unjustifiable.

Rightly understood, the above quotes portray some kinds of *dukkha* or suffering as characteristic of all forms of life. Hence, *dukkha* should not be understood only in a psychological sense to mean pain, misery, or suffering. As a technical term, *dukkha* means much more: it refers also to such ideas as imperfection, conflict, unrest, absence of an abiding substance, etc. Even the states of mental absorption (*jhāna*) are included in *dukkha,* for they too are subject to change. The Buddhist commentators recognize the wider implications of this term when they explain it as three-fold: *dukkha* as suffering or intrinsic suffering (*dukkha-dukkha*), *dukkha* as change (*viparināma-dukkha*), and *dukkha* as conditioned states or *dukkha* due to formations (*saṅkhāra-dukkha*).[10]

In early Buddhism mental culture plays an important part. Based on the Pali Canon, one is compelled to conclude that early Buddhism is realistic. There is no explicit denial anywhere of the external world. Nor is there any positive evidence to suggest that the world is mind-made or simply a projection of our subjective ideas. Throughout the teachings of the Buddha it is the language of realism that is encountered.

The Buddhistic view of reality is based on a doctrine of elements, an analysis of the world of experience into a number of factors. Only these basic factors are real. It is in the Abhidhamma that this doctrine of elements is expounded. These elements of existence are either mental or material, and in their combination they constitute the world of experience.

From what has been considered so far, it should be clear that early Buddhism accepts a realistic view of existence. To deny the reality of the world of experience is to deny the very basis of religious life; this would make the religious life meaningless also. According to Buddhism, therefore, the ethico-religious life has its very foundation in the reality of the empirical world.

Earlier Buddhism made no distinction between esoteric and exoteric teaching as Mahāyāna Buddhism did; it did not encourage the idea that one should postpone attaining *nibbāna* in the hope that one would thereby be enabled to remain in *saṃsāra* and help others in the path of sanctification. It emphasized, rather, the personal endeavor to win enlightenment—it was a *kathiṇayāna,* a difficult career or path, which promised no blissful heaven. The Mahāyāna thinkers nick-named this difficult path *hinayāna* because no saint (*arahat*) had any higher objective than his own salvation, and the objective of a follower of *hinayāna* was to be an *arahat* as quickly as possible. *Arahatyāna* is, therefore, from the viewpoint of a Mahayanist, a little vehicle (*hinayāna*) which can only carry one passenger safely across the stormy sea of life; *bodhisattva-yāna*, on the other hand, is the great vehicle (*mahā-yāna*) because in the capacious boat—the heart—a saint can ferry other souls across the dangerous flood of *saṃsāra*. For this compassionate attitude Mahāyāna Buddhism could curtail what it felt to be the serious as well as narrow aspects of Hinayāna Buddhism.

It has been suggested that a better distinction without indicating reproach of any kind between the two forms of Buddhism could be made by their geographical locations, viz., Northern and Southern Buddhism. Ceylon, Burma, and Thailand are strongholds of Southern Buddhism, while Nepal, Tibet, China and Japan constitute the home of

Northern Buddhism. Southern and Northern, Hinayāna and Mahāyāna, flourished side by side and even in the same monastic establishments. But later on the followers of the Buddha could introduce greater innovations into Northern Buddhism than into Southern Buddhism, which strictly confined itself to three baskets (*piṭaka*) of sacred literature: the discourses of the Buddha (*sutta*), the rules of monastic discipline (*vinaya*), and the higher philosophical teachings (*abhidhamma*).

Early Buddhism ordinarily means Buddhism which claims as the source of its doctrines the Pali Canon. The Pali Canon, on the evidence upon which this consideration is based, is not a book but often a verbal, socially approved collection which took its shape or came into existence in stages. It grew up stage by stage with additions and alterations. Just as the taste of sea water is salty, no matter which part of the sea is tasted, just so deliverance (*vimutti*) of consciousness, as prescribed in the Pali Canon, is the underlying pervasive religious sentiment. "*Vimutti* is indeed the reason or central interest which gives a new character or tone to the whole of the corpus of texts composing the Pali Canon."[11] Thus, this deliverance (*vimutti*)—the free state of mind which follows upon attaining the sense of peacefulness of the entire being—was experienced for the first time by the Buddha in that age. *Vimutti* is the central point of interest, so far as the purely spiritual aspect of Word of the Buddha (*Buddha-vacana*) is concerned.

Within deliverance there arises a psychological or psychical aspect, without which appreciating one cannot realize the spiritual aspect. *Nibbāna,* which constitutes the central core teaching of early Buddhism, is another name for *vimutti*. Early Buddhism broadly speaks of two aspects of *vimutti* (1) *ceto-vimutti* and (2) *paññavimutti,* i.e., (1) deliverance of the mind and (2) deliverance through wisdom. "The stepping-stone to either is *sīla*—a term which comprehends the whole of humankind's moral sphere of existence and behavior."[12] *Sīla*, *samādhi*, and *pañña* are the three main factors of the entire system of which the ultimate aim is the attainment of deliverance.

Samādhi comprehends 'concentration,' as the mental state of being firmly fixed on a single object. *Pañña* or *vipassana* comprehends the whole of our rational sphere of existence. The path of *samādhi* in Pali is called *samathayāna* or a path to tranquillity. One who follows the path of *pañña* only is called *vipassanayāni,* a follower of the path of knowledge. The highest ideal is to fulfill both the paths. One who fulfills the path of *vipassanayāna* is called *paññavimutta* (emancipated by way of wisdom or insight). One who fulfills *paññavimutti* really fulfills both.

Hence, it is obvious that hard spiritual exercise is needed to attain this ultimate goal, *nibbāna*. Without a certain measure of concentration, calm or insight cannot be developed, and without some measure of insight no concentration can be developed. They are inseparable. In summary it can be said that the three-fold training, virtue (*sīla*), concentration (*samādhi*) and wisdom (*pañña*) lead to complete mental purity and final deliverance. It is therefore important to understand how our latent tendencies and defilements function.

7

The Process of Thought in Later Buddhist Schools

Due to the various interpretations of the master's original words along with the wide and rapid spread of his teaching, not only in the country of its birth but also outside, in the course of time there arose within Buddhism a great divergence of views among its followers. The various views falling under later Buddhism are broadly classifiable under two heads, going by the names of Hinayāna and Mahāyāna. These terms are variously explained, the most common explanation being that they signify respectively the "small way" and the "great way" of salvation. *Yāna* also means vehicle, *maha* means great, thus the Mahāyāna is the great vehicle or vessel, in which ultimately all living creatures will be carried along to salvation. It is clear from the inferiority indicated by the word *hina* (small or low) that the names were devised by the followers of Mahāyāna. Of these, Hinayāna had the earlier origin; but the distinction between the two is not merely one of chronology. They differ in their philosophic and ethical outlook as well. For instance the adherents of Hinayāna believe in the reality of outward objects—however they may conceive of reality itself—and are for that reason often described in the Hindu works as Sarvastivādins, while the adherents of Mahāyāna adopt the opposite view. Another important difference is that while the Hinayāna is content to stop at pointing out the means for the individual to release himself from the bondage of *saṃsāra,* the Mahāyāna teaches that the awakened individual should work without resting, for the spiritual welfare of the world.

In short, with regard to the reality of the world the Hinayāna holds a psychological realism, the Mahāyāna regards it as illusion. Consequently, the Hinayāna regards suffering as real, the Mahāyāna as an illusion. Such radical differences between the two forms of the doctrine in essential matters have led some to suggest that the Mahāyāna has been influenced by alien thought, as there were foreign incursions into India during the formative stages of this phase of Buddhism.

Several Buddhistic works of this period (ca. 150 B.C.E.) are written in Sanskrit. Some of them are probably renderings from Pali originals, which shows that Buddhism gradually assumed a more and more scholastic character. But this should not be taken to mean that it ceased to exist as a popular creed. Buddha preferred to dwell upon the practical aspect of his teaching, refusing to dwell upon the theory underlying it. All the different shades of philosophic theory—realistic and idealistic—are found within Buddhism itself. Hence, Hiriyanna says, "philosophy repeated [itself twice over in India—once in the several Hindu systems and again in the different schools of Buddhism."[1]

A vast body of literature began appearing as early as the first or second century C.E. and constitutes the beginning of the later phase of Buddhism. I can refer here only to a small portion of it, remarking, by the way, that several of the works in Sanskrit have been lost. The literature reflected the development of two distinct schools and many sub-schools. Due to diverse opinions and the clash of ideas, the classical Buddhist system became rich and mature.

The main branches of Hinayāna are: Sthaviravāda (Theravāda), Sarvastivāda, Vaibhāsika and the Sautrāṅtika. The Vaibhāsika and the Sautrāṅtika are elaborately discussed by the non-Buddhist writers as they are mainly based on philosophical speculation and therefore are important in relation to the development of Hindu thought. The Hindus also discussed the Sarvastivāda because it also involves metaphysical discussions mainly based on epistemological ground.

Under the idealistic form of Mahāyāna, the two important schools (Yogācāra, the subjective idealists, and the Mādhyamika involving Śunyavāda) are discussed by the non-Buddhist writers because of their philosophical importance. The Sarvastivāda derived its name from the doctrine that affirms existence at all times, with the past and future events equally existent in the present. In their acceptance of existence at all times, it seems that the Sarvastivāda exhibits a tendency to compromise toward the theory of permanence in their acceptance of existence at all times. Hence the criticism offered by Sankara (8th century C.E.) in his *Brahma Sutra Bhāṣya* against the Buddhist momentariness is most applicable to Sarvastivāda and not to Theravāda.[2]

The Sarvastivādins met the objections toward the "existence at all times" by replying that, just as the same woman may be called mother, daughter, wife, and so on, so the same entity may be called present, past, or future in accordance with its relation to the preceding or the succeeding moments. When the Hindu writers refer to the Buddhist doctrine in general, they refer to the Sarvastivādins, by which they mean both the Sautrāṅtikas and the Vaibhāsikas, ignoring the difference that exists between them.

The Vaibhāsikas are the direct realists who hold that the external world is an object of perception. They accept the reality of both mental and non-mental phenomena. The *Abhidhamma* treatises formed the general foundation of the philosophy of the Vaibhāsikas. They followed exclusively a particular commentary, *Vibhāsa* (or *Abhidhamma Mahavibhāsa*). In Yamakami Sogen's own words: "Vaibhasikas or Adherents of the Vibhasa (or Commentary on the Abhidharma) attached themselves exclusively to the Abhidharmapitaka and, generally speaking, they refused to accept the authority of the *Sutrapitaka* and the *vinayapitaka*.[3]

One of the most interesting facts that is derived from the special commentary of the *Vaibhāsika (Abhidhamma Mahavibhāsa)* is the meaning of the word "Abhidhamma." It is called by that name "because it examines all dharmas,"[4] the prefix "abhi" being in the sense of "about or concerning." In Buddhaghosa's opening chapter of the *Aṭṭhasālini,* it is said that the word *Abhidharma* means "*Dharma* par excellence." But this explanation is not quite as satisfactory as that of the *Mahāvibhāsa-śāstra* which settles the doubts completely.

The Sautrāṅtikas are also realists like the Vaibhāsikas, but they are representationalists or critical realists. The main difference between the two is that while the Vaibhāsikas hold that the external world is perceived directly, the Sautrāṅtikas affirm that it is known by inference. This view of the Sautrāṅtikas was criticized by the Vaibhāsikas on the ground that the external world is the direct object of our experience through the senses, hence, such direct sensible experience is as clear as daylight. According to the Vaibhāsikas, the Sautrāṅtikas, due to their theory of inference, are contradicting their own position, for, in that case, knowledge is always an experience, and as such, open to doubts. Hence on this supposition, there can be no distinction between valid and false perception.

One of the most remarkable thoughts of the Sautrāṅtikas is their theory of continuum (*santati*) of a person or a thing in cosmic ground-consequent process. Of course, this theory of continuum of persons and things in cosmic situations is not a new theory, for in the Sāṃkhya system also, an individual living being is interpreted as a constituent of the three *guṇas* or qualitative processes in relation. But there is a difference between the Buddhist view of the presented universe as ground-consequent continuous process (nature)—which is phenomenological—and the Sāṃkhya view of the universe as evolved from the basis of *Prakriti*—a transcendent, persistent process in a state of disequilibrium.

Another difference between the Vaibhāsikas and the Sautrāṅtikas is that the Vaibhāsikas maintain the continuous existence of the past, the present, and the future as real. If the past were not real, the action done in the past would not produce the fruits in the present. The Sautrāṅtikas contend that the Vaibhāsika doctrine of continuity of time involves the heresy of eternalism. The Sautrāṅtikas on the other hand deny the reality of the past and the future and affirm the reality of the present moment alone. They maintain that entities emerge from non-existence, they exist for a moment, then they disappear.[5] Things are momentary. The present alone is real. The past and future are unreal. The Sautrantika school developed the doctrine of impermanence into that of "momentariness." Everything by its very nature is perishing. There is no cause in the past as producing a thing's destruction. A thing exists for one moment only and then vanishes.

It appears that the Vaibhāsikas have doctrinal similarity with the Sarvastivādins in their affirmation of the existence of all times, past, present and future, while the Sautrāṅtikas have similarity on the same aspect of reality of present only with the Theravadins. The difference between the Sautrāṅtika and Theravāda is that, while Sautrāṅtika acknowledges the authority of the *sutra,* Theravāda acknowledges the authority of the *Abhidhamma.* Like Theravāda, the Sautrāṅtika school also criticizes the Sarvastivāda. The Sarvastivāda reject the authority of the *sutras* altogether and acknowledge only the *Abhidhamma.* Therefore, their philosophy is known as *Abhidhamma* only.

The Sarvastivāda can claim to be as old as the Theravāda with which it has close doctrinal affinity. Both Theravāda and the Sarvastivāda hold that the whole reality is composed of elements. These *dharmas* are irreducible elements. All things mental and physical are produced by the elements. Both believe in *anattā* of persons *(puggala nairatmya).* Both believe that what is known as an individual is the combination of five aggregates (*pañcakhandha*) which is temporary. Both believe that the goal is *nibbāna,* which is attainable in this very life if ignorance (*avijjā*) which is the root-cause of the aggregate condition resulting in suffering (*dukkha*) can be removed. For the cessation of suffering, a path has been prescribed which consists of the Eightfold Noble Path (*aṭṭhāṅgamagga*); this can be reduced to the triadic path of *sīla, samādhi*, and *paññā*. Its pure ethical character in the Buddhist sense has already been clarified.

According to both the Theravāda and Sarvastivāda the cause of suffering is something psychological. Concerning spiritual progress, both schools recognized the different orders of persons in the path towards enlightenment (*nibbāna*); these persons are: *sotāpanna* (a stream winner), *sakadāgāmi* (once returner), *anāgāmi* (never-returner), and *arahat* (fully enlightened).[6]

The speculative schools attached to the Hinayāna belong to both Sarvastivādins and Theravādins. They are the exponents of a transcendent atomistic pluralistic realism of a sort, having a faith in many transcendental flashes of intuition, or *dhammas*. The Sarvastivādins (Hinayāna) give a list of seventy-five *dharmas*, while the Vijñānavādins (Mahāyāna) list one hundred *dharmas*. According to Yamakami Sogen, the *Abhidharma* of the Sarvastivadins forms the stepping stone from Hinayāna to the Mahayāna philosophy.[7]

Vasubandhu, the author of the *Abhidharma-Kośa*, says that mind is called *cittaṃ* because it observes, it considers and it discriminates. So the words *cittaṃ* (also *manas* and *vijñāna*) are in a certain sense synonymous in the Buddhist psychology. Mind (*cittaṃ*) is the king of the mental realm (*caitta dharo*).

The Sarvastivādins made six subdivisions of minds, which are technically called "the six kinds of *vijñānas*." The Sarvastivādins recognized forty-six kinds of *citta-dharmas* (*Caittasikas*). The Vijñānavādins who also classify them differently, give a list of fifty-one. While according to the Theravāda *Abhidhammatha-saṅgaha*, there are fifty-two *caitta-dharmas* or mental properties.

The Sarvastivādins divide the *caitta-dharmas* (also called psychic levels or transcendental flashes) into six classes, and they broadly cover the bases of all orders of psychic processes from the apparent to the transcendental.[8] They are stated below by way of explanation.

(1) *Mahābhūmika dharma*, the first in the above list, is the mental operation which as its name indicates, is common universally to a human's mental functions in the moral and immoral realms. These are ten in number, viz., (1) *vedanā* (sensation), (2) *saṅjñā* (conception), (3) *cetanā* (motive), (4) *sparsa* (contact), (5) *chanda* (conation), (6) *mati* (intellect), (7) *smriti* (memory), (8) *manasikara* (attention), (9) *adhimokkha* (determination), (10) *samādhi* (concentration).[9] They cover the whole sphere of experience from the apparent to the transcendental order, from sensation to concentration.

The above factors are almost similar to the factors which are present in *sabba-citta-sādhāraṇa cetasikā* of Theravāda *Abhidhamma*, such as *phassa*, *vedanā*, *saññā*, *cetanā*, *manasikara*, and *ekaggata* which is the same as the *samādhi* of *Mahābhūmika-dharma*.[10] These two factors, *chanda* and *adhimokkha*, are similar to the *pakinnaka cetasika* (particular mental factors).[11]

Mati (intellect), which is the same as *paññindriya* (or reason as a guiding principle) is a psychic factor which is present only in those types of consciousness that are very much thoughtful.[12]

Smriti (memory) is the same as *sati* (mindfulness) of *sobhana-sādhāraṇa-cetasika.*[13] *Samādhi* is the same as *ekaggatā* (concentration upon an object).[14]

(2) The next heading is *kusala-mahābhūmika-dharma* which, as the name indicates, are mental operations common to all good thoughts, and are ten in number: [1] *sraddhā* (faith), [2] *viriya* (diligence), [3] *upekśā* (indifference), [4] *hri* (shame for one's self), [5] *apatrapa* (shame for another), [6] *alobha* (freedom from covetousness), [7] *advesha* (freedom from hatred), [8] *ahiṃsā* (harmlessness), [9] *prasrabdhi* (peacefulness of mind), and [10] *apramāda* (carefulness).[15] They belong to *dharmas* of upper orders of experience.

The above *kusala mahābhūmika dharmas* are quite similar to the *sobhana sādhāraṇa cetasikas* of Theravāda Abhidhamma such as *sraddhā*, *hri* (shame for one self), *alobha* (freedom from covetousness), *adveṣa prasrabdhi* (peacefulness of mind, *adosa passadhi), appamāda* (carefulness, which is the same as mindfulness), *upekkhā* (indifference). They have been included in the group *sobhana-sādhāraṇa* as *adosa* (good will).

Viriya (diligence) is included in *pakinnaka cetasika* (particular mental factors). *Ahiṃsā* (harmlessness) corresponds to that of rectitude of mind which is *sobhana-cetasika* (wholesome mental factors).

(3) The third heading is *klesa-mahābhūmika-dhamma*, which arise with *klesa,* that is to say, when any kind of passions begin to arise. They are six in number: [1] *moha* (ignorance), [2] *pramāda* (inattention or carelessness), (3) *kausidya* (indolence, sloth or laziness), (4) *asraddhā* (absence of faith), (5) *styana* (idleness), (6) *auddhatya* (rashness and thoughtlessness).[16]

These *klesa mahābhūmika* are quite similar to the *akusala-cetasika* (unwholesome mental factors) of the Theravāda. But they differ in number. They are fourteen in number, whereas *klesa mahābhūmika dharma* are six in number.

(4) Next comes the *akusala mahābhūmika dharma* which arise with the activities of the mind that are evil. They are two in number: [1] *ahrikata* (shamelessness for oneself), and [2] *anaprtapa* (shamelessness for another).[17] These are included under the *akusalacetasikas* of Theravāda Abhidhamma.

(5) The next heading is *upaklesa-bhūmika-dharma.* These *caitta-dharmas* are not common to all *klesas* when they arise, but spring up

only in company with the six defiled *vijñāna*, namely: *mano-vijñāna*. *Upa* indicates their limitation. They are ten in number, namely, *krodha* (wrath), *mraksha* (hypocrisy), *matsarya* (envy), *irshyā* (jealousy), *paritāpa* (anguish), *vihiṃsā* (injury), *upanāha* (enmity), *māyā* (flattery), *satya* (trickery), and *mada* (arrogance).[18]

These factors are almost more or less a repetition of *akusala cetasika* (unwholesome mental factors) of Theravāda. The eighteen *caitta dharmas* of *klesa bhūmika, akusala bhūmika,* and *upaklesa bhūmika* correspond to the fourteen factors of *akusalacetasika,* except for four extra-evil factors—hypocrisy, injury, flattery and trickery—which are nothing but mere repetitions of immoral factors which are already included in *akusalacetasikas.*

(6) Lastly are the *aniyata-bhūmika-dharma*, which do not fall within a definite or particular division or *bhūmi*. They are eight in number, such as: (1) *kaukrita* (repentance), which is similar to one of the Illimitables of Theravāda psychic factors; (2) *middha* (torpor); (3) *māna* (pride); (4) *pratigha* (anger); (5) *vicikiccha* (doubt) which are also found in *akusala-cetasikas*; (6) *vitarka* (discussion), (7) *vicāra* (judgment), are also included in *pakinnaka cetasika* in the Theravāda school.[19] According to *suttanta,* these two factors always go together. But Abhidhamma holds that *vicāra* can be separated from *vitarka*. In the second stage of *jhāna* (absorption) according to Abhidhamma, *vitarka* is excluded, *vicāra* exists independent of it. They differ in strength in different types of consciousness. In the *jhāna* they are stronger. They are present both in the moral and immoral types. In the last *aniyata-bhūmikā-dharma, rāga* (affection) has been already included in the group *sobhana-sādhāraṇa* as *adosa* (good will) which have been taken from the four-fold *brahma-vihāra*.

Thus, forty-six kinds of *caitta dharmas* (psychic processes or bases from the apparent to the transcendental orders), while they are treated in general as psychic flashes or dharmas by the Sarvastivādins, they have been included among the fifty-two *cetasikas* of Abhidhamma. The Sarvastivādins divide the *caitta-dharma,* into six classes with the six divisions of mind.

The Theravāda Abhidhamma divides the *cetasikas* (psychic conditions) into: (1) *Sabba-citta sādhāraṇa*—universal factors common to all types of consciousness. They are seven in number. (2) *Pakinnaka* (particular properties) which are six in number. (3) *Akusala* (unwholesome factors) are fourteen in number and the same as *akusala-mahabhumikas*. (4) Then there are nineteen *kusala* (wholesome) factors which are present in moral or good consciousness and rooted in *alobha, adosa and amoha*. These mental factors demonstrate that the good states of consciousness are light, calm and peaceful. These have been also mentioned in *kusala-mahā-bhūmikā-dharma*. 5) The three *viratis* (abstinences), such as: right speech, right action, and right livelihood are not mentioned in the *Abhidharma Kośa*. (6) The two illimitables, compassion and joy, are also included in *kusala-mahā-bhūmikā-dharma*. (7) *Pannindriya* or reason as a guiding principle is the same as *mati* of the *mahā-bhūmika dharma*. The *cetasikas* of the Sarvastivādins and the Theravādins are almost the same if viewed from the transcendent-apparent levels and orders. The difference between the two is superficial; the divisions are the same with different names, terms and number. The same kind of superficial differences are found regarding the stages of sanctification of Mahāyāna and Hinayāna.

The most difficult task of an adept *(yogāvacara)* both in Hinayāna and Mahāyāna is the fulfillment of the condition laid down for passing from the state of *puthujjana* (a world being, one who has not eradicated any of the ten fetters)[20] to that of an *ārya* (a human capable of attaining the highest knowledge). The Mahāyānists demand that one must develop *bodhicitta* (Buddha-nature) before one can be entitled to commence the practices of *bhumis*, while the Hinayānists hold that one must first understand the Four Noble Truths and have faith in the teachings of the Buddha, and then one will be able to enter the stream *(sota)* of sanctification—the Noble Eightfold Path.

According to the teachings of Very Venerable Taungpulu Kaba-Aye Sayadaw, an adept, by complying with the rules of *adhiśīla* (training in higher morality) becomes a *sotapanna* (a streamwinner) and can also achieve *sakadāgāmi* (once-returner; the adept becomes an *anāgāmi* (never-returner) by complying with the rules of *adhicitta* (training in higher mental life), and he becomes an *arahat* by complying with those of *adhipanna* (insight into things based on higher wisdom).[21] The Hinayāna system does not offer any parallel to the first *bhumi* of the Mahayānist's *pramudita* (joyful), for it has no concern with *bodhicitta*.

The second *bhumi-vimala* (pure, free from impurity) corresponds to the *sotāpatti* (stream-winner), and *sakadāgāmi* (once-returner) of the Hinayāna. Under the practice of *sīla,* he realizes the *akusala kamma* (immoral acts) of the beings and therefore he conducts them to the *kusala patha* (good paths), so that the beings may be free from the disastrous results of unrighteous conduct. Also they become *savaka* or *ariya-puggala* (noble disciple), *pacceka-Buddha* (silent Buddha), Bodhisattvas and the Buddhas.

The third *bhumi - prabhākari* (light-giving, luminous, illuminating), corresponds to *anāgāmi* (never reborn) of the Hinayānists, whereby the practice of eight *jhānas* (trances) the four *brahma-vihāras* (the four subtle moods), and six *abhiññas* (higher spiritual powers) leads one to the realization of the real nature of things and existence. The Bodhisattva also realizes that things are subject to causal law. He realizes that things are impermanent, full of suffering, have momentary origin, that they decay, that things are without beginning and end. The fetters of *kāma* (lust), *rūpa* (form), *bhāva* (becoming) and *avijjā* (ignorance), having been destroyed, bring about the cessation of *rāga* (greed), *dosa* (hatred), and *moha*, (delusion).

In Hinayāna, an adept, after completing the *sīlas* (morality), attempts to rise higher and higher in the training of mind through *samādhi* (concentration). The *Visuddhimagga* also tells that an adept, after completing the *citta* practices, becomes an *anāgāmi* (never-returner), i.e., he will not be reborn in *kāmadhātu* (the sensuous world). Thus it is clear that the Hinayāna *anāgāmi* stage is parallel to the Mahāyāna third *bhumi* of *prabhākari* or *adhicittavihāra*.

The practices of the fourth *bhumi-arcismati* (radiant), fifth *bhumi-sudurjaya* (very difficult to conquer), and sixth *bhumi-abhimukhi* (face-to-face), correspond to the *abhipanna* (practices of higher wisdom) of the Hinayānists. According to the Hinayānists an adept, upon completion of the *pañña* practices, becomes an *arahat,* an Enlightened One.

With the sixth *bhumi,* the comparison of the Hinayāna and Mahayāna stages ends. The accounts of the remaining four *bhumis* have nothing to do with Hinayāna practices. These four *bhumis* are: seventh *bhumi-durangama* (far-going, far-reaching), eighth *bhumi-acala* (immovable, steadfast), ninth *bhumi-sādhumati* (stage of good thoughts) and tenth *bhumi-dhammamegha* (cloud of the doctrine, cloud of virtue). Up to the sixth *bhumi* one realizes the *puggala-sūnyata* (devoid of personality). Here the comparison with Hinayāna ends as they have nothing to do with *dharma-sūnyata* (devoid of things). According to the Mahāyānists, from the seventh bhumi the Bodhisattva commences the attempt to realize the *dharma-sūnyata.* Here, after completing the seventh *bhumi* by acquiring immeasurable knowledge, the Bodhisattva realizes the true nature of things: *dukkha*, *anicca*, and *anattā*. He is now a member of the Buddha family. It is after the tenth *bhumi,* that a Bodhisattva becomes a *tathāgata* (the Perfect One, literally, "the one who has thus gone, or thus come"). The *bhumi* is called *tathāgata bhumi.*[22]

In the Hinayāna literature one does not expect any account corresponding to that of the last four *bhumis*. They avoid all the metaphysical conceptions introduced by the Mahāyānists, though they cannot offer a treatment similar to the devotion-inspiring stories of the lives of the Bodhisattvas. In their literature the Hinayānists tried to prove that a Buddha is a "rare being" and superior to the men and the gods, but they also mentioned that there is hardly any distinction between an *arahat* and a Buddha, except that the latter is a founder and teacher of religion. There is really no objective way to measure spiritual levels. Though there are many spiritual paths, there is but one goal, and this has been called different things by the different seers. *"Ekam sad vipra bahudha vadanti,"* truth is one; the wise speak of it in many ways.

In all the various religious discourses of the most Venerable Taungpulu Sayadaw of Burma, there is one simple emphasis: "Stop thinking; do it." This message will certainly kindle a light in the deepest recesses of the heart of the meditator, a light which will not only dispel darkness, but one which will also add a new impetus for practice rather than for discursive thinking. Gradually, the sad, shaky house of craving, hatred and delusion will transform into an attractive house of *saddhā* (faith), *hiri-ottappa* (moral shame and moral dread), and *sati* (mindfulness), and thereby it will take a firm foundation. For this psychological transformation to occur, considerable amounts of patience and discipline are necessary. If it were so easy to achieve enlightenment, then enlightened beings would be a dime a dozen. Perfect balance between *samādhi* (concentration) and *viriya* (energy) is needed.

As mentioned, Mahāyāna Buddhism is divided into two systems of thought: the Mādhyamika and the Yogācāra. The Mādhymikas were so called on account of their emphasis on *madhyama-pratipat* (the middle view). In his first sermon at Benares, the Buddha preached the middle path, which is neither extreme asceticism nor extreme sensualism. However the middle path, as advocated by the adherents of the Mādhyamika system, is not quite the same. Here, the middle path stands for the non-acceptance of the two views concerning existence and nonexistence, eternity and non-eternity, self and non-self, and so on. In short, it advocates neither the theory of reality nor that of the unreality of the world, but merely of relativity. It is, however, to be noted that the middle path propounded at Benares has an ethical meaning, while that of the Mādhyamika is metaphysical in content (though not in a strict conceptual sense: concepts are avoided by systematic elimination, "neither this nor this...").

The founder of this school is said to be Nāgārjuna, who was born to Brahmin parents in South India about the 2nd century AD:

> Most of the Japanese and Chinese scholars of Buddhism deal with the Yogacara school before the Madhyamika school, as a more convenient and more systematic exposition of Buddhist philosophy...I do not find, however, any reasons...to depart from the chronological order. I shall therefore treat of the Madhyamika before I take up the Yogacara school.

> Moreover, according to the opinion accepted by the Buddhist scholars in general, Asvagosha is the twelfth patriarch while Nagarjuna, who is said to have been born in Southern India, 700 years after Buddha's death...is the fourteenth patriarch, Deva, a native of Southern India or Ceylon, who is the greatest of the disciples of Nagarjuna is the fifteenth patriarch.[23]

To the scholar of Buddhism, no part of the subject is more difficult and more interesting than to fix the date of the founder of Mahāyāna. In general, Nāgārjuna is said to be the founder of it; but if the *Mahāyāna-Sradhotpada Sastika* is a work of a Bodhisattva Asvagosha who is well known as the author of *Buddhacarita*, we must acknowledge the latter be the greatest pioneer of Mahāyāna Buddhism, being the predecessor of both Nāgārjuna and Asaṅga. At any rate, one cannot be far wrong in deciding the probable date of Nāgārjuna from the data furnished by Fufatsan-yin-yuen-kwhan, concerning the life of Nāgārjuna from the catalogue of Nanjio.

In his famous work, *Mādhyamika Śāstra,* Nāgārjuna states, with great dialectical skill and scholarship, the philosophy of the Mādhyamika school. Nāgārjuna claims to have inherited from Buddha Sākyamuni his fundamental doctrine of interdependent causation which was embodied in the truth of voidness and in terms of a dialectic of neither/nor; nonappearance and non-disappearance; non-cessation and non-eternity; non-identity and non-differentiation; non-coming and non-going forth. The *Mulamādhyamika Śāstra* by Nāgārjuna consists only of verses and was commented on later by scholars of the Mādhyamika school; hence some details will be useful for present deliberations. Why Nāgārjuna explained interdependent causation as non-appearance, non-disappearance, and so on, will be considered here very briefly. The truth of interdependent causation means "that things exist, interdependent and relative to each other," and the notions of the "appearance" of things is denied.

Accordingly, the appearance of things does not mean the appearance of any substantial things, nor can there be things that might be taken as disappeared or being destroyed. Thus the notion of destruction is also denied. Thus, the truth of interdependent causation of things implies non-appearance and non-disappearance.

According to the theory of interdependent causation, it is inconceivable that there can be any "active subject" which might act of its own accord. In other words, the "subject of a substantial action" is denied by this theory, and there can be "no action" such as coming or going which might be conceivable as the action of a subject with substance. Therefore, there is non-coming and non-going forth.

Furthermore, the theory of interdependent causation does not admit that a constant cause develops in continuous succession into the effect which is identical with the cause, nor that an effect exists apart from a cause which has ceased to exist. Therefore, the truth of interdependent causation implies the possible suggestions of non-identity and non-differentiation, non-cessation and non-eternity in causal relations, but not in any definite sense.

Accordingly, the standpoint of interdependent causation is incompatible with the notion of the "phenomenal world" emerging from an anti-phenomenal active cause, such as *prakriti,* as claimed by the Hindu Samkhya system, which advocates the theory of evolutionism or the interconnection between cause and effect—a theory which holds that the phenomenal world is latent in *prakriti* and is destined to emerge from it. Hence a conclusion can be drawn that the subjective mind as well as objective matter acquire a concrete significance not in any positive sense, in the light of the theory of interdependent and interrelated causation and that they reveal their true character only when viewed as non-identical and non-differentiated, non-interrupted, and non-eternal in dialectic ways of "neither/nor." Nāgārjuna gives several instances to show that a concrete significance in dialectic negations is gained if the "subjective and objective," the "internal and external," the "active and passive" are recognized as co-related forms to be excluded. For instance, he argues in the tenth chapter of the *Mulamādhyamika Śāstra* in the following way:

> Fire does not exist in relation to kindling; and fire does not exist unrelated to kindling.
>
> Fire does not come from something else; and fire does not exist in kindling. The remaining [analysis] in regard to kindling is described by [the analysis of 'that' which is being gone to, 'that which is gone to' and 'that which is not yet gone to.'
>
> Fire is not identical to kindling, but fire is not in anything other than kindling.
>
> Fire does not have kindling as its property; also the kindling is not in fire and vice versa.[24]

This argument enables one to conclude that the truth of interdependent and interrelated causation does not imply any relationship between two concrete things, one preceding and the other following, but some unseen or inconceivable process which can be meditatively determined by a freedom from all intellectual propensity in positive aspects—it is possible only by an act of the dialectic of neither/nor, which posits nothing, but which includes all views dialectically.

To sum up, Nāgārjuna gives the fundamentals of his philosophy in a nutshell. He describes *pratitya-samutpāda* (dependent origination) by means of "eight negatives." There is neither origination nor cessation, neither permanence nor impermanence, neither unity nor diversity, neither coming in nor going out, in the law of *pratitya-samutpāda*. Essentially, there is only non-origination which is equated with *śūnyata* (emptiness). In the *Mādhyamika Śāstra,* Nāgārjuna says, therefore: "The fact of dependent origination is called by us *śūnyata*. There is no dharma [character] of things which is not dependent on some other condition regarding its origin. Therefore, there is no dharma which is not *śūnya*."[25]

This view is called the middle *(madhyama)* path, because it avoids extreme views by denying, for example, both absolute reality and absolute unreality of things and asserting their conditional existence. This was the reason why Buddha called the theory of dependent origination the middle path. And so Nāgārjuna in his *kārikā* says that Śūnyavāda is called the middle path because it implies the theory of dependent origination. In other words, Nāgārjuna does not deny the existence *(bhāva)* of things *(dharmas)*. He does not also affirm the opposite *(abhāva)* of the *dharmas;* he denies also the self-existence *(svabhāva)* of things, and by excluding all possible intellectual forms by dialectic negations he advocates the *śūnyata* (emptiness) of the formal intellectual ways. On the basis of this emptiness of intellectual forms he could prepare the ground for the transcendent psychic conditions of the following: no suffering *(dukkha), no karma, no Nirvana,* not even the Buddha. In his *Mādhymika Kārikā,* Nāgārjuna says that there is no self-existent producer (*kartā*), product (*karma*), and producing (*krīyā*). "The producer proceeds being dependent on the product, and the product proceeds being dependent on the producer."[26] What one has to observe is only relativity and nothing else, but only if one stays in the sphere of apparent experiential process and doesn't cultivate meditation in dialectic ways to rise to the condition of placidity.

One should not misunderstand Nāgārjuna's denial of the self-existence *(svabhāva)* of the Buddha, *Dhamma* or *Nibbāna*, as he argues in his *Mādhyamika kārikā*. He is a logical interpreter of the Buddha's teaching of the Middle Path or the *madhyama mārga*. By *śūnyatā,* therefore, the Madhyamika does not mean absolute non-being, but relative, and also the sphere of the apparent universe of *Pratitya-Samutpāda* (dependent origination). The Mādhyamika view holds *śūnyata* transcendent and as a condition of freedom from all possible intellectual forms by a dialectic negation—neither/nor—to be the central idea of its philosophy and designated the *śūnyavāda,* thought not in any positive sense.

The *Mādhyamika-kārikā* further deals with two kinds of truths: *saṃvritti* (conventional or empirical truth), and *paramārtha* (higher or transcendental truth). The former refers to ignorance or delusion which envelops reality and gives a false impression while the latter is the realization that worldly things are non-existent like an illusion or echo. *Paramārthasatya* (transcendental truth) cannot be attained without resorting to *saṃvrittisatya* (conventional truth). *Saṃvrittisatya* is only a means, while *paramārthasatya* is an end. In his *Mādhyamika-kārikā,* Nāgārjuna talks about the Buddha's teaching in relation to these two truths:

> The teaching of the Buddha of the dharma has recourse to two truths: The world-ensconced truth and the truth which is the highest sense.
>
> Those who do not know the distribution (vibhagam) of the two kinds of truth do not know the profound 'point' (tattva) in the teaching of the Buddha.
>
> Emptiness, having been dimly perceived, utterly destroys the slow-witted. It is like a snake wrongly grasped or [magical] knowledge incorrectly applied.[27]

The doctrine of *śūnyavāda* has been understood in India as nihilism by non-Buddhist philosophers in general, to mean that the universe is totally devoid of reality, that everything is *śūnya,* or void. Hence by defining the two kinds of truth, the conventional or the mundane, and the transcendental or the ultimate, in his *kārikā,* Nāgārjuna clears up the misunderstanding of Nihilism stamped on his Buddhist philosophy of *śūnyatā.* He does not introduce any new tenets, yet his dialectical approach to the goal of ultimate reality takes a new vista. The principle of relativity or non-absolutism is the same. The ultimate goal of *Nibbāna* is the same. The empirical world or the *saṃsāra* is also the same. The method is different. One is meditative and the other is intellectual. Where the Buddha applies the method of intuition for the realization of the ultimate, the *Nibbāna,* Nāgārjuna follows the dialectic method for the understanding of the ultimate. Nāgārjuna removes all the obstacles of dogmatic attachments and orthodox faiths from the ultimate reality.

According to T.R.V. Murti, this Mādhyamika philosophy of *śūnyatā* is the central philosophy of Mahāyānism. In his book, *The Central Philosophy of Buddhism*, Murti says:

Sunyata (Doctrine of the Void) is the pivotal concept of Buddhism- The entire Buddhist philosophy turns on this. The earlier realistic phase of Buddhism, with its rejection of substance and uncritical creation of a theory of elements, was clearly a preparation for the fully critical and sub-conscious dialectic of Nagarjuna. Not only is the Yogacara idealism based on the explicit acceptance of *Sunyata*, but the critical and absolute trend in the *atma* tradition is also traceable to this.[28]

Scientifically, Nāgārjuna's theory of dependent origination or *pratitya-samutpāda* leads one beyond the spatio-temporal causality of the universe. Nāgārjuna bases the world on the absolute ground of *śūnyatā*. All phenomenal things are absolutely interdependent. Dr. A.K. Sarkar writes on Nāgārjuna's interlinked phenomena: "To Nagarjuna, the relative existence is borrowed existence, it is not a real existence, just as the borrowed money is not real money. The world of relativity invariably suggests a transcendent "undifferentiated existence or experience."[29]

The dialectic of Nāgārjuna which denies all the existing realistic and idealistic views of the universe is considered to be the philosophy of the Copernican revolution. As the Copernican revolution proved that it is the earth that revolves around the sun and not the sun around the earth, so also the Mādhyamika philosophy of Nāgārjuna interpreted the reality of Buddhism as *śūnyatā* which exists in the middle of the two extremes of eternity and annihilation and not vice versa.

According to T.R.V. Murti, "like the Advaitism of Sankara, the Mādhyamika is a revolutionary interpretation of Buddhism. It deepened Buddhism by analyzing fully its implications."[30] The Mādhyamikas, therefore, hold that there is a transcendental reality (noumenon) behind the phenomenal one and it is free from change, conditionality and all other phenomenal characteristics. That reality is void. The word "void" is not entirely fitting and is often misleading, yet if we look for another word there will be none better. It is, after all, an idea dialectically established. It is nameless *(akhyāti)* and characterless *(alakṣaṇa)*. It is simply the negation of an independent reality or the negation of specific character.[31]

While agreeing with the Mādhyamikas as to the unreality of external objects, the Yogācāra school differs from them in holding that the mind *(citta)* cannot be regarded as unreal. For them all reasoning and thinking would be false if the mind itself was unreal, and the Mādhyamikas could not even establish that their own arguments were correct if this were not the case. To say that everything, mental or nonmental is unreal, is suicidal. The reality of the mind should at least be admitted in order to make correct thinking possible. The mind, consisting of a stream of different kinds of ideas, is the only reality. The objects perceived are all ideas in the mind. The existence of any external reality cannot be proven, because it cannot be shown that the object is different from the consciousness of the object.

The Yogācāra school is another important branch of the Mahāyāna, and was founded by Maitreya (3rd century, C.E.), Asanga (4th century C.E.), Vasubandhu (4th century, C.E.), Sthiramali (5th century C.E.), Dinnaga (5th century C.E.), Sandraksita (8th century C.E.), and Kamalasila (8th century C.E.) were noted teachers of this school. The school reached the acme of its power and influence in the days of Asanga, and his brother Vasubandhu. The name Yogācāra was given by Asanga while the term Vijñānavāda was used by Vasubandhu.

The Yogācāra was so called because it emphasized the practice of *yoga* (meditation) as the most effective method for the attainment of the highest truth *(bodhi)*. All the ten stages of spiritual progress *(dasa bhumi)* of Bodhisattvahood had to be passed through before *bodhi* could be attained.

The Yogācāra view is also called Vijñānavāda, or idealism, because it admits that there is only one kind of reality which is of the nature of consciousness *(vijñāna)*. It holds *vijñapti-mātra* (nothing but consciousness) to be the ultimate reality. In short it teaches subjective idealism or that thought alone is real. In Dr. Takakusu's words:

> I prefer to use the term ideation-store. The ideation-store itself is an existence of causal combination, and in it the pure and the tainted elements are causally combined or intermingled. When the ideation-store begins to move and descent to the everyday world, then we have the manifold existence that is only an imagined world ....It is only from the Buddha's Perfect Enlightenment that pure ideation flashes out.[32]

> According to the Samdhinirvocana Sutra, the Sutras on which the realistic doctrine of Abhidhamma is based are called 'the first wheel of the law'; the Prajnaparamita Sutras on which Nagarjuna's nihilistic teaching is founded are named 'the wheel of the law' without characteristic, and the same dhinirvocana and the other sutras which give a basis for the Yogacara position are said to be 'the last wheel of the law' which synthesizes the realistic and

nihilistic views. It gives an explicit explanation of the voidness and substancelessness of all things, while the second wheel of law, the wheel of the law without characteristic, suggests the same idea only implicitly. This is what is called 'the division of the Buddha's teachings into three stages.'[33]

The Yogācāra brings out the practical side of philosophy, while Vijñānavāda brings out its speculative features.[34] The *Laṅkāvatāra Sutra,* an important work of this school, maintains that only the mind *(citta mātra)* is real, while external objects are not. *Citta mātra* is different from *ālaya-vijñāna* (a storehouse). The mind considered in its aspects of being a storehouse or home of all impressions is called by Vijñānavādins *ālaya vijñāna.* According to Yamakami Sogen: "There is difference between the two *ālaya.* One is the relation of suchness to all things, or that of noumena to phenomena is expressed by *Ālaya-vijñāna* which must be differentiated from the word *ālaya-vijñāna* in relation to Vijñānavādin school which indicates relative knowledge."[35]

According to Vijñānavādins all things in the universe similar to the classification adopted by the Sarvastivādins, are divided into two groups, viz., composite *(sanskrita),* and uncomposite *(asanskrita).* The former is subdivided into four classes; *cittam, caittam, rupam* and *citta-viprayukta-saṅskāra dharmas.* "The number of *dharmas* which are counted as seventy-five by the Sarvastivādins, is reckoned as 100 in this school of Vijñānavāda."[36] There are ninety-four composite dharmas such as *citta-dharma* (8), *caitta-dharma* (51), *rupa-dharma* (11), nonmental (24). Then there are six kinds of *Asanskrita dharma* (incomposite). Thus there are altogether 100 dharmas. All these dharmas, with the exception of incomposite dharmas, are the effects of the mind.

In the Buddhist psychology, the word mind is variously termed as "*cittaṃ,*" "*manas,*" and "*vijñāna.*" The three are the same in their origin, but are used differently to denote the three different aspects of *cittam. Cittam,* according to Vijñānavādins, means: 'attending' and 'collective.' By 'attending' [is meant] consideration of objects to which the attention has been attracted, while collecting means 'impressions about the objects' which has impressed the mind.[37] *Manas* also has two significances: "thinking" or "considering." By thinking is meant a kind of sub-consciousness, which has for the object of its contemplation, egoism.[38]

Vijñāna has also two meanings: "discriminating" and "perceiving." Discriminating means differentiation between the outward manifestations of the objects which form the subjects of contemplation, while "perceiving" is the perception of the objects in the external world, which causes us to experience sensation (sense-objects).

Caitta dharma means mental attributes. *Cittam* and *caitta dharma* are very often compared in Buddhist philosophy to a king and his ministers. For, just as ministers follow the king whenever or wherever he goes, in the same way, whenever *cittam* acts, *caittam* necessarily succeeds.

Rūpa-dharma is the activity of the mind expressed through physical sense-organs and the objects affected by them. The term *viprayukta-saṅskāra-dharma* includes whatever is non-*caitta* and non-*rupa*—connected with neither the material nor the mental domain. "*Asanskrita Dharma* denotes the state in which birth and death cannot exist; it is noumenon of the universe which is unchangeable, limitless and incorporeal; it is of course free from the Law of Birth and Death. In simpler words, Asanskrita expresses a "state of suchness."[39] Hence *cittam* is the basis or repository of all things mental and material.

The mind, as the home of all latent ideas, is called *ālaya-vijñāna*. It may be regarded as the potential mind and answers to the soul or *ātman* of other systems, with the difference that it is not one unchanging substance like the soul, but is a stream of continuously changing states. Through culture and self-control this *ālaya-vijñāna* or the potential mind can gradually stop the arising of undesirable mental states, and develop into the ideal state of *nibbāna*. Otherwise, it only gives rise to thoughts, desires, attachments which bind one more and more to the fictitious external world. The mind, the only reality according to this school, is truly its own place, it can make heaven of hell and hell of heaven. In Sogen's own words:

> Thus that which leads us to the realm of enlightenment or *Nirvana* is *Alaya-vijnana,* and that which makes us wander about and lose ourselves in the illusory world or *Samsara* is also *Alaya-vijnana.*[40]

> The term Yogacaras tempts me to make a little digression. The term denotes that these practitioners of Yoga in India had arrived at the theory of the *Alaya-vijnana by* experience rather than by reasoning...Here, one is reminded of the psychological researchers which are being pursued so eagerly today in Europe, Japan and America. Perhaps, the science has been reserved for perfection one day or another in this very land which was the first garden where the tree of psychological science blossomed forth and bore the two

> noble fruits of the orthodox *atman* and the Buddhistic *Alaya-vijnana*.[41]

In the psychological world, the *Ālaya-vijñāna* is the name for the sum total of the normal consciousness and sub-consciousness.

8

A Comparison of Early and Later Schools of Buddhist Thought and Western Psychology

It has been said that while school after school of epistemological and ontological inquiry arose, the practical aspect of Buddhist teachings remained almost unchanged. This is very well applicable to early schools of Buddhism, but not to the later schools. The belief that all is suffering and that sensual pleasure itself is "attenuated pain" continued to characterize the later doctrine, as did the belief that right knowledge was the means of overcoming it. The course of discipline laid down for the attainment of *nibbāna* was also the same as before—partly moral, partly intellectual—but the conception of the ideal of life was vastly transformed.

The Vedic period gave rise to two ideals which influenced the evolution of early and late Buddhist schools: that of action *(pravritti)* which insisted on strict adherence to vedic ritual; and that of contemplation *(nivritti)* which is quietism, which demanded an escape from life of rites and rituals in order that one may devote oneself entirely to contemplation. Early Buddhist schools (Hinayāna) adopted the latter, while the later Buddhist schools (Mahāyāna), largely under the influence of Hindu thought, modeled its practical teaching on the former. Although saving oneself still continued to be the aim of life, it ceased to be commended for its own sake and came to be regarded as but a qualification to strive for the salvation of others. This is the ideal of the Bodhisattva who, having perfected himself, renounced his own salvation for the spiritual good of others; it is distinguished from that of the Arahat of the earlier Hinayāna schools. Through the centuries the two ideals became more and more distinct and strengthened the separatism of the early and late schools; this is unfortunate because, as described in both the *Buddhavaṃsa* and *the Nidāna-Kathā*, the Bodhisattva path is essential to the Hinayāna practitioner who wishes to become a Buddha.

Burmese Buddhism (Theravāda) provides a living example of how the arahat path to sainthood is still pursued today. There is much respect for a *tawya* monk, meaning one who lives in the remote forest all by himself with no connection to the world around him. A *tawya* or a hermit is never lonely. He is happy in the forest with the meadow for his bed, the rock for his couch, the shady tree for his dwelling, cool water from the waterfall for his drink, flowers, fruits and berries for his food, and the birds and deer for his companions.

Thus, it is really difficult to measure the spiritual goals, as both are "ends" in themselves, from two different yet important attitudes towards one's life and towards the lives of others. One may refer to some kindred modes in Mahāyāna and Hinayāna, though not related to philosophic thinking. In this connection one may compare in some aspects the view of mind as held by the Mahāyāna school and the Theravāda school of Buddhism.

The mind considered in its aspect of being a storehouse or house of all impressions is called by the Vijñānavādins (the later schools of Mahāyāna Buddhism) as *ālaya-vijñāna*. Like the *ālaya-vijñāna*, the potential mind of the Vijñānavādins, there is the *bhavaṅga sota* of the Theravādins (earlier schools of Buddhism).

> A flow of the momentary states of subliminal consciousness of a particular class constitutes the bhavanga sota, the stream of being, bounded by birth (*patisandhi*) and decease (*cuti*). And as decease is but a prelude to another birth, the continued flow of the stream of being from life to life, from existence to existence, constitutes *samsara*, the ocean of existence.[1]

Bhavaṅga is the subconscious continuity of organic life. Consciousness springs out of the subconscious and lapses into the subconscious again. This continuous life-force is one, though there may be different *vithis* (roads) at different times of our conscious life and the *cuticutta*, the *patisandhi* are but different names for some particular movements of the flow of *bhavaṅga* which is continuous.

This main flow can be stopped if ignorance (*avijjā*) can be rooted out through good *karma*.

It is very interesting to note how the Hinayāna studies of *dhamma* passed on to Mahāyāna *dharma*, through the Satyasiddhi school of Harivarman, a native of central India who lived in 253 C.E. He was the chief disciple of Kumaralabdha, a teacher of a Hinayāna school in Kashmir. Some maintain that he adhered to the Hinayāna doctrine with the help of the Mahāyāna. The Sarvastivādins maintained the soulessness of an individual (*ātma nairatmya*) though not of things. Harivarman maintained the *nairatmya* of both persons as well as things, as characteristics of the Mahāyāna. According to Harivarman, the exponents of "all-is-void" are the direct antagonists of the Sarvastivāda standpoint with regard to everything, if "strenuously denying the absolute existence of anything in the transcendental sense."[2]

Harivarman formulated his views in his work, *Satyasiddhi Śāstra* or *Treatise on the Demonstration of the Truth.* The very name of the school has been forgotten in India, so it will not be out of place to say something about the author Harivarman and his *Śāstra*. The great critical work of the free-thinker Harivarman appeared at a time when the so-called Hinayānists and Mahāyānists were hotly discussing the claims of their respective schools that they be regarded as representatives of genuine Buddhism.

From the opening words of his *Treatise on the Demonstration of the Truth*: "Now, I am going to uphold the meaning of the Sacred Canon in its real truth, because every Bhikkhu of every school and Buddha himself will be hearing my exposition."[3] The universe contains eighty-four *dharmas* (elements), which also are void of any abiding reality. He advocated the theory of two kinds of truth—conventional truth *(saṃvritti satya)* and ultimate truth (*parmārtha satya*), and held that *ātman* exists conventionally, but not ultimately.

Harivarman accepted the Hinayānist theory of the *Buddha-kāyā* and explained *dharma-kāyā* as being five-fold, consisting of conduct *(sīlā),* concentration *(samādhi),* wisdom *(prajñā),* deliverance *(vimukti),* and knowledge and insight into deliverance *(vimutti, jñāna darśana).* He, however, believed in the special powers of the Buddha. This school contends that only the present is real, while the past and the future have no real existence.

According to Harivarman, the classification of the universe into eighty-four elements also is real only as a conventional truth, not as the ultimate truth. From the conventional point of view, there is negativism which denies the existence of matter *(rupa),* mind *(citta),* and mental properties *(caitta-dharmas)* which are neither matter nor mind, and even of uncreated dharmas. From the point of view of supreme truth, there is total nihilism (*sarva-śūnyatā*). In fact, Harivarman's doctrine is to be regarded as the highest point of philosophical perfection attained by Hinayānism and, in a sense, it constitutes the stage of transition between the Hinayāna and the Mahāyāna.

The oldest school of Hinayāna Buddhism is the Sthaviravāda (Theravāda) or the Doctrine of the Elders. The Mahāyānists claim that the Buddha gave them higher teaching because of their capability, and say that Hinayāna philosophy was the Buddha's way of adapting the full teaching for the less qualified disciples. The Theravāda tradition is often equated with Hinayāna Buddhism, but in fact, it is only one of at least eighteen Hinayāna schools. It is, however, the only one that has survived.

It is clear from what has been said so far that early Buddhism is realistic and the later schools of Buddhism are idealistic. There is apparent resemblance between the Buddhist realist who assumes, like Kant of Western philosophy, the "thing-in-itself." But the two views are not the same, since the Buddhist realists assume that the "thing-in-itself" is known through the disciplines of mind, whereas for Kant, it is "unknown and unknowable" by its very nature. Hence "realism" or "idealism," even if used as philosophic parlance, has distinctiveness in the Indian cultural contexts.

The habit among many Western as well as Eastern scholars is to associate the Buddha's teaching with that of some Western philosophical systems, such as Existentialism, Logical Positivism, etc., and a few go as far as to compare Buddhism with the philosophy of David Hume.

The Buddha's remarkable teaching to the Kalāmas—that a person should believe a thing to be true when he has personally tested the truth of it, and finally has satisfied himself that it is true—led a few scholars to compare the anti-metaphysical attitude of the Buddha with the anti-metaphysical attitude of the Logical Positivistic thinkers. Because of the Buddha's scrutinizing spirit, though, he was not dogmatic on even this most fundamental teaching—the path of free inquiry.

In the history of philosophy, there are alternate periods of construction and deconstruction. Logical Positivism is the peak of the destructive phase of the cycle. And again, if one attentively analyzes the Positivists' criticism of metaphysics, one finds that it is nothing more than tautology. (By considering only empirical statements to be meaningful, and, hence, all metaphysical statements to be totally meaningless, the Logical Positivists neatly exclude from their "scientific" system all non-empirical matters and, hence, the bulk of philosophical inquiry, including the practical foundation of

Buddhism—ethics.) The Buddha always refused to answer any metaphysical questions because he knew that they do not tend toward anything profitable, but only to continued speculation. Whenever a logically-minded critic ventured to ask him whether an *arahat* exists after death, whether he does not exist or whether he is both in existence and non-existence, the Buddha answered by noble silence—out of his triadic discipline of *sīla* (conduct), *samādhi* (meditation), and *pañña* (insightful understanding). Where the Logical Positivists stuck with words, the Buddha realized that arguments can be futile word games. He emphasized detachment from such intellectual modes of understanding.

There is a remarkable affinity, though, between Existentialism and Buddhism. Existentialism is a revolt against the denial of one's basic existence as a person. "Existentialism does not boast of a clear-cut system or philosophy in any traditional sense."[4] "Existentialism is a combined philosophy and psychological attitude choosing life and revolt rather than doctrine or grace. Its very choice of apparent pessimism is its redeeming feature."[5] In this aspect of pessimism one can find general affinity between Buddhism and Existentialism: "In the existential current of the West and the Buddhistic current, there is temperamental affinity, though there may not be any affinity in the details of their speculative current."[6] "Existentialism crystallizes the present sense of intellectual and moral need. It is a passionate return of the individual to his own freedom...in the unfolding of its processes, to extract the significance of his being."[7]

Existentialism is a real awakening not only for the Western but also for the Eastern peoples. A human comes to occupy a central place in reality. A person is not merely a spectator of the universe. He realizes or seeks to realize certain ends and purposes which have objective validity. Hence, like Buddhism, Existentialism is a psychological attitude with a quest for values; but the Buddha's quest in the Indian cultural background was the quest for *Dhamma* (Truth), which needs, as indicated above, a strenuous discipline in meditative ways. With so much affinity between Existentialism and Buddhism, there is still a world of difference between the two. There is a sense of responsibility, no doubt, in the Existentialist philosophy, but it surely lacks the meditative attitude and indicators for transformation found in Buddhism. As the saying goes, an ounce of practice is far superior to tons of theories. Existentialism cannot eliminate the discursive mode completely.

9

Summary and Conclusions

Gotama Buddha's first and foremost concern was to eradicate suffering. After immeasurable effort he discovered that the gradual cessation of ignorance breaks apart the links in the whole chain of suffering. He is said to have become the Buddha by means of this two-fold contemplation: in the presence of ignorance, suffering arises; with the cessation of ignorance, suffering fails to arise, up and down the chain of causation. Then, what is this ignorance? It is a lack of right insight. Insight into what? This became an issue in the development of the concept of the dependent origination in later days. At the outset the development of insight means the attempt to understand the five aggregates of clinging as impermanent, unsatis-factory and without self.

In Buddhism, the entire stress is on the mode of living, on the righteousness of life, on the removal of defilements (*kilesa*). A merely theoretical proposition, such as "there is no self," would be regarded as utterly futile. All Buddhists follow the Buddha in wanting to learn how to lead a selfless life, and not indulge in mere metaphysics. To lead a selfless life, the most important quality is to have an affectionate veneration for the Triple Gems—the Buddha (the Enlightened One), the *Dhamma* (his teaching), and the *Saṅgha* (the Noble Order)—and to have an earnest desire to tread on the path as laid down by the great seer. It is undoubtedly a disciplined way of life as described, and not a stand on speculative metaphysics.

The light of Asia as manifest in the supreme personality of the Buddha rayed out, through the centuries and throughout the world. He was the perfect embodiment of knowledge, courage, love and sacrifice, whose heart overflowed with purest emotion on seeing that human life was essentially fraught with misery and pain and that behind the superficial momentary glow of sensual pleasure there lay the misery of old age, sickness and death. He was moved by that spectacle and sought a remedy for men's ills. At the age of twenty-nine, he kicked away gold, lust, and fame, the three universal fetters of man, and within six years he found enlightenment. Dispelling the dark clouds of ignorance and conquering *Māra* (the Prince of Evil), the Buddha preached the truth he had discovered, without distinction of caste, creed or gender. Thus Buddhism was embraced by the rich and the poor, the high and the low, the intellectual and the dull, alike. The teachings spread, far and wide, from his homeland to Ceylon, Burma (now called Myanmar), Siam (Thailand), Malaya, Java, Sumatra, and then again to Nepal, Tibet, Mongolia, Korea, China and Japan. It became a world religion and a great cultural force through the lengths and breadths of the vast continent of Asia.

The Buddha was primarily an ethical teacher and a social reformer. Hence, the Buddha exhorted his disciples first to establish themselves in virtue or moral habits before entering on the path of meditation and wisdom, as mental purity and attainments are not possible without moral purity. To reach the goal one will have to avoid the two extremes of sensualism and extreme asceticism, and follow the middle way (*majjhima-patipāda*); and by emphasizing universal love, charity, tolerance, compassion and mindfulness, one can pave the path towards liberation. The Buddha's ethical "middle path" avoids the two extremes of self-indulgence and self-mortification equally.

Buddhism consists of many philosophical schools and has produced a vast literature. The Buddha's teachings have always been and will continue to be interpreted, amplified and elaborated by his disciples. He referred to a number of metaphysical views prevalent in his times and condemned them as futile. Whenever metaphysical questions were put to him, he avoided them, saying that they were neither profitable nor conducive to the highest good. Philosophy (in the sense of abstract discourse) purifies none; peace, through disciplined psychological attitudes, does.

The tendency to split and diversify itself into schools and sub-schools appeared very early in the history of Buddhism. Religiously Buddhism is divided into two important streams—Hinayāna and Mahāyāna. Hinayāna relied on the words of Buddha: "Be a light unto thyself" (*ātmo dīpo bhava*), emphasizing liberation for and by the individual himself or herself. It is a difficult path of self-help. Its goal is to become an Arahat, the one who has attained salvation by killing the enemies of greed, hatred, and delusion through personal effort.

Nibbāna is regarded as the extinction of all misery, including the passion for discussion. Mahāyāna, the Great Vehicle, the big ship which can accommodate a much larger number of people and can safely and securely take them to the shore of *nirvāṇa* from the troubled waters of the ocean of *saṃsāra,* refers to earlier Buddhism as Hinayāna, the small vehicle. The idea of liberation in early Buddhism or Hinayāna is said to be negative and egoistic. Mahāyāna believes that *nirvāṇa* is not a negative cessation of misery but a positive state of bliss by rightly understanding the vacuous character of discursive tendency and subjecting it to thorough analysis and then eliminating its core by dialectic negations. Its ideal saint is the Bodhisattva who defers his own salvation in order to work for the salvation of others, knowing fully the emptiness of any definite stand. The Bodhisattva is he who attains "perfect wisdom" by knowing the vacuity of all intellectual propensity, ever dwelling in it, and inspired by the love of all beings, ceaselessly working for their salvation which is to be obtained here in this world. He is ready to suffer gladly, so that he may liberate others, cherishing no fixed standpoint.

The Mahāyānists are proud of their faith as a progressive and dynamic religion which throbs with vitality. It has the capacity to adapt itself with the changing environmental conditions. They believe in the Triple Body (*Trikāya*) of Buddha, that is, (1) *Dharmakāyā,* the Law body, (2) *Saṃbhogakāyā,* the bliss body, and (3) *Nirvāṇakāyā,* the transformation body—the dynamic triadic currents—*Trikāyā.* The early Hinayānists conceived the Buddha in terms of *Rūpakāyā*, the human body, and *Dharmakāyā*, the collection of *Dharmas*. It was a first glimpse of glory to be dynamically oriented later on.

The Hinayānists recognize the four stages of spiritual progress: *sotapatti* (a stream winner), *sakadāgāmi* (once-returner), *anāgāmi* (never-returner) and *arahat* (the fully awakened one, or the killer of the mental defilements) The Mahayanists recognize ten stages of progress through which a Bodhisattva passes in order to have complete emancipation and become a Buddha, in the sense of *trikāyā,* with dynamic liberal attitudes.

I have endeavored to study the process of Buddhist thought in some important early Buddhist schools and also some later Buddhist schools, from the Buddha's psycho-ethical attitude and from Western philosophy in general. The effort here has been to present an adequate background of Buddha's fundamental teachings from which further investigation of Buddhist ethic-based psychology can be carried on.

Here it should be pointed out that Buddhist teaching advocates non-violence, and this non-violence is to be exercised towards one's own mind as well as towards the external world. To repress natural desires is merely to force them below the surface of consciousness where they are liable to develop into morbid obsessions, eventually to break out in hysteria or other psychological disorders. Buddhism does not favor this rough treatment of the psyche, which has produced so many undesirable results in Western monasticism. Instead of repression,

Buddhism affords disciplined, meditative methodology, with effective techniques of attenuation and sublimation.

Techniques of meditation (*bhāvanā*) in Buddhism are designed for specific ends, according to the personality of the meditator, and for the purification of an individual undisciplined psyche. They are selected by the teacher with the requirements of the individual in mind. From the beginning, the Buddhist system of self-training makes a radical readjustment within the mental processes, so the personality is molded anew by the triadic discipline of *sīla* (moral conduct), *samādhi* (concentration), and *paññā* (wisdom).

Among all the Buddhist schools, the Theravāda claims to be closest to the psycho-ethical attitude of the Buddha. My contention is that all the schools, small or big, are just vehicles (*yānas),* avenues on the same path. Hence, all are important in one way or another. The Buddha's doctrine is called the "vehicle" in the sense that it is like a ferry boat. To enter the Buddhist vehicle means to begin to cross the river of life by stepping off the shore which is ignorance. The teachings can be compared to rafts—when the goal has been attained, they become useless. Just as differences in shape, weight and material among rafts does not really matter, so differences in teachings also do not matter. This point of view is set forth both in Theravāda and Mahāyāna Buddhism. Hence, instead of the names *Mahāyāna* and *Hinayāna,* there should be *Buddhayāna* or *Buddhadhamma*—to express a comprehensive attitude which may be developed through both Hinayāna and Mahāyāna Buddhism.

Thus Buddhism for all sects, as already noted, is nothing but "the path leading to release" (*nibbānagamana-magga*) from the normal tendency to experience and discuss in restricted ways, which foster specific arguments, theories and systems. Buddhism is a dynamic current raising humanity to a condition of freedom from all metaphysical propensities, to a disciplined meditative way of life which is utterly free and completely without tension.

Appendix A

Practical Abhidhamma

One day a woman who taught meditation, psychology and Tai Chi came to meet the Very Venerable Taungpulu Sayadaw. This professor, being a meditation instructor, had read quite a bit about the Abhidhamma and tried her best either to teach or give talks on depth psychology from the Abhidhamma perspective. She began by talking about the Abhidharmakośa, the Mahāyāna psychology. Very Venerable Taungpulu Sayadaw was calm as ever but also surprised. First of all, he was surprised that a meditation instructor could be so restless. She started boasting to Sayadaw that she had studied in Japan, Thailand, and Burma to learn Abhidhamma. She felt Abhidhamma is important for its therapeutic benefits which are very helpful to Western students. I became nervous when she opened a fruit basket she had brought to offer to Venerable Taungpulu Sayadaw. But instead of offering the fruit, she took out the oranges, apples, bananas, etc., and asked him, "What will you call these?" Venerable Taungpulu Sayadaw looked at me and said, "What is she doing? Why is she showing me all this fruit? We get every kind of fruit in Burma." I told her that Sayadaw said these fruits were available in Burma. She became more restless and said, "I just wanted to know whether you would differentiate between reality and concept." When I translated this to Sayadaw he asked me to tell her, "Eat some of this fruit, and then meditate." This was Sayadaw's first step to teach her Abhidhamma, that is, eat to your satisfaction, then you can be calm, and can meditate; only then can you really begin to see. Further, she asked Sayadaw, "What books do you recommend?" Sayadaw replied, "No books. The real teaching is to open the heart, and the hardest thing in this world is to open the closed heart." As a result of this situation, Taungpulu Sayadaw requested me to write about Abhidhamma in very simple language and emphasize its practical side.

In this hectic modern age, there is tension and restlessness everywhere. We are robbed of that calm and quiet which is so important for our mental well-being. The percentage of unhappy people in our modern "civilization" runs high. Some believe that the high incidence of personality disorders is a new phenomenon, directly related to modern life itself. We don't have to look too far to see how these disorders can arise: feelings of insecurity are pervasive, stemming from a sense of instability engendered by excessive competition in commerce and industry, the fear of nuclear war and waste, the phenomenal pace of the advancement of technology, and the striving to "keep up" socially and financially with others. In the search for a way to relieve these emotional disturbances, three keywords have appeared: psychology, yoga, and meditation. Surprisingly, we find that meditation, once assumed to be the exclusive property of the East, has now come to the West—and in a big way. It is such a joy to see this growing new interest in meditation. Even psychologists recommend meditation as mental therapy. So, we see that meditation cannot be the exclusive domain of any particular discipline or doctrine. If we investigate the matter, we will find that meditation is actually a part of the prime roots of every religion, philosophy or system of yoga. Meditation exists in the early traditions of every culture precisely to transcend thinking, and to develop understanding. Meditation, then, is a universal tool, the means by which we can directly examine, understand and tame our own mind.

There are two main purposes to meditation practice. The first is to learn to still the mind, to calm ourselves. It is surprising but true that simply by cultivating calmness we can overcome most of our emotional or psychosomatic problems and anxiety disorders. Developing calmness through meditation is the practice which tranquilizes and humbles the mind, making it clearer and brighter, until it is empty and radiant. In this way, a new mind is uncovered, a "right mind" which is powerfully simple, creatively silent, energetically still.

But tranquillity is not the entire answer. If we hope to make any changes in our pattern of life or society, if we wish to fulfill our duties and obligations to fellow human beings, then we must also have understanding. And so we come to the other main purpose of meditation: to learn to understand oneself, and thereby to understand others.

Today we analyze everything, evaluating and re-evaluating, continually trying to adjust ourselves to this changing world. In our search for happiness, we try to understand life as best we can. We may even practice psychological analysis, in order to understand ourselves intellectually, and perhaps emotionally. But still, we remain far, far away from the goal. Might there be a better kind of understanding? One that will lead to true happiness and peace?

To get beyond the intellect, to go beyond emotions, means to practice meditation. Meditation is the development of face-to-face awareness of your own mind and body. The process of meditation is a transcending of the intellectual mind, since the intellectual mind itself becomes an object of awareness. As a result, the understanding that arises from this direct awareness is very different, fundamentally different, from intellectual understanding. We might call it "intuitive understanding." It is clear, directly apparent, independent of discursive thinking and other forms of mental clinging. And it is this understanding that can bring happiness and peace.

It is true that the intellect may be responsible for many of the changes and improvements in our modern world. In the endless work going on, scientists are pursuing experiments upon experiments, and the results are startling. But all these improvements, though they have their advantages and rewards, are by their very nature material, external, subject to change and further change. How can stillness and peace be found in this way?

Though science may help us to understand the external world, the understanding of the world within science may not be of much use to us. The scientific method might reveal some of the secrets of the brain, studied as an object of hypothesis and experimentation; but to reach a subjective understanding of one's own mind, isn't it absolutely necessary that the mind turn to reflect on and observe itself? To understand the world within, we need to cultivate our own mental faculties through meditation.

And so it is natural that our quest for peace and self-understanding should bring us to self-examination through meditation. But where does one begin? If we just sit down and close our eyes, tranquillity and peace are not likely to appear on the spot. According to the teachings of the Buddha, what we need to do first is to cleanse our speech, thought, and actions. As the Buddha pointed out, "For a long time has man's mind been defiled by greed, hatred and delusion. Mental defilements make beings impure; mental cleansing makes them pure."[1]

This cleansing process, in Buddhism, begins with moral conduct (*sīla*). Only on a firm foundation of *sīla* can we build up a stable structure of concentration (*samādhi*), and so make way for the arising of intuitive insight or wisdom (*paññā*). A person who practices meditation while being heedless of his moral conduct will find no end of strange occurrences happening to him. This is because clarity of mind depends directly on self-honesty, and self-honesty only has the courage to emerge when one's actions are pure, benevolent, harmless, and blameless.

So, we say that we must begin with morality, but this does not mean that a *yogi* (meditator) must be completely moral, that is, free from all vices, before he or she begins meditation. To take this view would be to act like a person who wants to wait until the ocean becomes calm before taking a bath. This will be procrastination, not meditation. Rather, morality, concentration and understanding are all integral components of meditation, developing side by side, each one assisting the others. As it is said in the *Dīgha Nikāya*, "As hand washes hand, and foot washes foot, so does conduct purify wisdom, and wisdom conduct."[2]

The greater our understanding, the more tolerance, patience and compassion we will have. With pure understanding, we will always be ready to forgive, like the most benevolent parent or teacher. Though the children may behave poorly, still the parents and teachers are always compassionate and loving towards their children. Similarly, accomplished yogis, through great understanding, relate to the world with lovingkindness and compassion. Understanding generates compassion, which in turn compels one not to commit thoughts and deeds which are harmful to oneself or to others. So long as you do not understand offensive thoughts, words or deeds, you are bound to commit them. But when you can see, with understanding, the results of your own actions, then unwholesome conduct will fall away like dead leaves from a tree.

With a foundation of moral conduct, then, wisdom will begin to arise. We may see that all our psychological problems are rooted in ignorance (*avijjā*) and craving (*tanhā*), and that these dangerous poisons are simply conditions of the mind. We may see clearly the ways in which our own minds cause us problems. The mind which is deluded sees substance (*attā*) in insubstantiality (*anattā*) and permanence (*nicca*) in that which is impermanent (*anicca*). The mind which craves sees purity (*subha*) in the impure (*asubha*), and satisfaction (*sukha*) in dissatisfaction (*dukkha*). Clinging to the impermanent, trying to gain satisfaction from bodies that grow old and decay. How can we not have problems if we continue to see the world in such cloudy light?

But it is essential to realize that the understanding which is capable of purifying the mind and bringing peace is not the understanding of the intellect, not the rationality of discursive thinking. Intellectual understanding is in reality only theoretical, the act of clinging to a view, dependent upon the coming and going of elusive thoughts. The Buddha taught that if we look closely, we will see that our physical bodies are riddled with impurities (*asubha*). Intellectually, we can easily accept this. But still, in the morning, we will be combing our hair, trying to look beautiful! It is only when we find hair in our bowl of soup and feel the aches and pains of age that we get a glimpse of the Buddha's insight; now our understanding is no longer merely intellectual! The Buddha also warned his disciples against the pitfalls of mere book learning. Concerning an aspirant's endeavors, the Buddha admonished:

> Even if he recites a large number of scriptural texts, but, being slothful, does not act accordingly, he is like a cowherd counting the cows of others, he has no share in the religious life.
>
> Even if he recites only a small number, if he is one who acts rightly in accordance with the law, he, having forsaken passion, hatred and folly, being possessed of true knowledge and serenity of mind, being free of worldly desires both in this world and the next, has a share in the religious life.[3]

The Buddha was not satisfied with any theoretical mode or code of discipline besides one's own intense practice. Success in meditation, like anything worthwhile, requires patience, tolerance, forbearance, and effort. Practice is necessary.

Since the Buddha was a practical man, he tried to eliminate the habit of mental speculation. He instead endeavored to assist the genuine spiritual development of humanity by the unbiased expression of the results of his own experience, and nothing more. Therefore, no theoretical understanding can communicate the distinctive features of the teachings of the Buddha. By analogy, the Buddha once pointed out that the mere reading and studying of medical textbooks could never cure a man's disease. For the real cure, one has to know the proper medicine, and then take it. In this way, the Buddha stressed that his system was practical and not theoretical.[4] Practicality is undoubtedly the perennial flavor of the Buddha's teaching.

The Buddha, the peerless physician, never wanted anyone to waste valuable time on metaphysical questions which unnecessarily disturb their peace of mind. When Malunkyaputta put to the Buddha ten well-known classical questions on metaphysical problems and demanded answers, the Buddha's answer was super-practical.[5] He related that if a man was wounded by a poisoned arrow, the immediate task would be to extract the arrow and cure the man rather than raise such distracting questions as to who shot the arrow, who made the arrow, what his name and family might be. If such questioning went on, the man would surely die! Further, the Buddha explained that spiritual life does not depend on views which seek the origin and explanation of things because they are not conducive to detachment, cessation, tranquillity, deep penetration, and full realization—*nibbāna*.

It must be mentioned that the highest truth does not depend on mere academic intellectual development, but on practice that leads the follower to enlightenment and final deliverance. The teaching of the Buddha is qualified by the command, "*Ehi-passiko*," inviting all to "come and see."

We can free ourselves from all defilements without consulting a therapist. Begin by investigating the mind; it is the center of all progress. Vow to conquer your mind, then slowly and patiently bring it under your control. The Buddha is called the warrior, the conqueror, not because of any victory except conquering the mind. Just as when clouds are driven away by the wind, the sky becomes blue, so also when by some practice the defilements of the mind like sensual desire (*rāga*), ill-will (*dosa*), or delusion (*moha*), are dispelled, the mental sky becomes clean, dispassionate, filled with virtue (*sīla*), love (*metta*), and insight (*paññā*).

Now, to develop perfect mental health, where should one begin? The most important technique ever given by the Buddha on mental health is the cultivation of mind through mindfulness *(satipaṭṭhāna)*. *Sati* means mindfulness, and *paṭṭhāna* is establishment. We all know in general what mindfulness is. We all know that the practice of mindfulness makes us more and more alert, more and more precise, and more and more careful in whatever we say or do. We also know that the absence of mindfulness results in the occurrence of accidents and errors which frequently disturb our lives. In the recorded sayings of sages and philosophers, as well as in the books of modern psychologists, mindfulness is strongly recommended as a quality of mind which makes for efficiency in everything. The mindfulness meditation technique was rediscovered by the Buddha more than 2,500 years ago. The meditation which the Buddha practiced just before his enlightenment is also *satipaṭṭhāna*.

In the practice of mindfulness, there is no mystery or magic involved. Step-by-step training, under careful and precise guidance, assures steady, sure development. The obstacles one encounters come from the mind itself. Therefore, it is useful to have the utmost determination and a most courageous attitude to persevere in training through the inevitable confusion, boredom, restlessness, physical discomforts, and fear that will definitely come up. One must even confront the desire to escape the necessity of taming the mind.

The Buddha treated mindfulness as a special subject of mental culture (*bhāvanā*). This can be found in the Buddha's important discourse entitled *Satipaṭṭhāna Sutta*. There are many different things about which one can be mindful. In other words, the objects of mindfulness may be many. But the Blessed One chose to practice *ānāpāna-sati*, that is, mindfulness of in-and-out breathing. With the continued practice of mindfulness of in-and-out breathing, the yogi develops within himself a wonderful tranquillity during his meditation practice. Later on, this tranquillity can continue right through the day.

The Buddha laid great stress on the importance of practicing mindfulness continually. He said it was essential and that it should be applied to all things and activities and at all times. The Buddha gives a striking parable to communicate the importance of developing mindfulness. Suppose a man, fond of his life and not wishing to suffer or die, is asked by a crowd of people to carry a bowl filled to the brim with oil. Behind him, a man spills but a drop of oil, and off goes his head. "What do you think?" the Buddha asks, "Would that man be mindful or not?" The meaning the Buddha gives is this: the practice of mindfulness should be taken seriously, as if we were that man, as if our life depended on it. And the Buddha's message is neither abstract nor far-fetched. In truth, death follows us at every moment, waiting to rob us of life; exactly when, we cannot say. So, the practice of mindfulness, though seemingly simple, is in fact difficult and deep. As the Buddha says, "Though one conquers in battle a thousand times a thousand men, yet he is the greatest conqueror who conquers himself."[6] There is nothing higher than self-mastery.

When the awareness becomes sharpened, one proceeds to observe the changing nature of body and mind, and experiences the universal truths of impermanence, dissatisfactoriness, and insubstantiality, or soullessness. This is to say, one begins to see things as they really are, and not as they appear to be or as we would like them to be. In other words, the yogi comes to develop insight (*vipassanā*), having gained calm and concentration through mindfulness practice.

In the word *vipassanā*, the prefix *vi* denotes "special" or "extraordinary," and *passana* means "seeing." Thus, what is meant by *vipassanā* is a type of extraordinary seeing, that is, seeing things in their real perspective, which is to say seeing the three characteristics of all phenomenal existence: impermanence, dissatisfactoriness, and insubstantiality. It is this insight that helps the yogi get rid of all defilements and makes way for the unconditioned peace—*nibbāna*.

The process of self-purification by self-observation may sound easy or not very easy. But regardless, through one's own efforts and understanding, one may penetrate the deepest levels of the unconscious mind and learn how to eradicate the deepest, most hidden complexes.

The goal of meditation is to cause the arising out of unconditioned peace within. But the process of purification that unfolds during training also manifests as reduction of congestions, aches and pains—mental, physical and emotional. The primary purpose of meditation is not simply to cure physical diseases although through the mental purification of meditation many psychosomatic and physical diseases are often cured.

There was a time when many people thought that meditation was only for monks, hermits, ascetic yogis, or forest-dwellers. But, if one defines meditation as mental culture, then surely there should be no barriers at all with respect to race, color, class, occupation, or gender. The entire path to the end of suffering is a universal remedy for universal problems and really has nothing to do with any organized religion or sectarianism. For this reason it can be practiced freely by everyone, at any time, in any place, and will prove to be equally beneficial to one and all. It is a practice which develops positive, creative energy for the betterment of the individual and the society.

Meditation, then, can be understood like the cultivation of the land. When you cultivate land, first you must clear it of wild trees, then you must till it, then fertilize it, and sow the seeds. Similarly, when cultivating the mind, first you have to destroy all the coarser mental defilements like greed, hatred, delusion, pride, etc., with your enduring energy, patience and perseverance before you can sow the seeds of faith, or confidence, and understanding. In such a way, with your body and mind fertilized with virtue and concentration, wisdom will be sure to sprout and grow.

One might pose the question: "Does meditation really do what is so confidently claimed for it?" The answer is plain: try it yourself, instead of wasting time in verbal questioning. No better proof can one have than personal experience.

The Very Venerable Taungpulu Kaba-Aye Sayadaw of Burma always emphasized the importance and benefits of mental culture *(bhāvanā)*. In his discourse, "*Dāna, Sīla, Bhāvanā*," Sayadaw said that *dāna* (charity or generosity) is good, but that compared to *sīla* (moral conduct), it is definitely inferior. Even if one observes only five precepts—to abstain from killing, stealing, sexual misconduct, false speech, and indulgence in intoxicants—one will be making a *mahā-dāna*, a great charity. And, of course, *bhāvanā* is far superior to any kind of merit resulting from any kind of *dāna*. The Venerable Sayadaw teaches his disciples:

> If one doesn't realize the becoming and vanishing of mind and matter, even though he may live for a century, he is not worthy of living.

> If he realizes the becoming and vanishing of mind and matter, even though he lives for a day, he is much nobler than the one who lives for a hundred years without realizing them.[7]

It is hard, then, to over-estimate the benefits that come from practicing meditation or mental culture. According to the Venerable Taungpulu Sayadaw, the most prestigious person is not the one who is a walking dictionary, but the one who is complete in *sikkhās*, that is, the training of *sīla*, *samādhi* and *paññā*. These three factors are a must on the royal road to *nibbāna*. But we must bear in mind: to attain enlightenment, one will have to practice. No amount of reading, reciting or studying will bring true insight or the real release from suffering. By reading all the suttas, one may become a *paṇḍita*, and so attain intellectual eminence. Yet, from the practical point of view of true spiritual development, one would still be a baby.

End Notes

Introduction

[1]Bhadantacariya Buddhaghosa, *The Path of Purification*, Bhikkhu Nanamoli, trans., 3rd ed. (Kandy, Sri Lanka: Buddhist Publication Society, 1975), p. 71.

[2]Ibid., p. 1.

[3]Haridas Chaudhuri, *The Philosophy of Love* (New York: Routledge & Kegan Paul, 1987), p. 9.

[4]Ibid., p. 9.

[5]Lord Horder, "The Hygiene of a Quiet Mind," Trueman Wood Lecture delivered before the Royal Society of Arts, 1938).

[6]Majjhima Nikaya, *The Middle Length Discourses of the Buddha*, Bhikkhu Nanamoli and Bhikkhu Bodhi, trans. (Boston: Wisdom Publications, 1995), p. 254.

Chapter 1

[1]Tittila, U Aggamahapandita, *Essential Themes of Buddhist Lectures* (Rangoon, Burma: Department of Religious Affairs, 1987), p. 71.

[2]Piyadassi Thera, *The Buddha's Ancient Path* (London: Rider & Company, 1964), pp. 15-17.

[3]Maha-Nidanasutta, *Dīgha Nikāya*, 11, 55.

[4]Nyanaponika Thera, *Abhidhamma Studies* (Kandy, Ceylon: Buddhist Publication Society, 1965), p. 8.

[5]Nyanatiloka Mahathera, *Guide Through the Abhidhamma Pitaka*, (Kandy, Ceylon: Buddhist Publication Society, 1971), p. 114.

[6]Nyanaponika Thera (1965), p. 2

[7]Ananda K. Coomeraswamy, *Buddha and the Gospel of Buddhism* (London: Harper and Row, 1964), p. 279.

[8]Dr. Herman Oldenberg, *Buddha: His Life, His Doctrine, His Order*, trans. William Holy (Varanasi, India: Indological Book House, 1971), p. 219.

[9]S. Radhakrishnan, trans., *The Dhammapada* (London: Oxford University Press, 1966), p. 59.

[10]U Thittila (1987), p. 140.

[11]Nanamoli Bhikkhu, *The Life of the Buddha According to the Pali Canon* (Kandy, Ceylo: Buddhist Publication Society, 1978), p 108.

[12]A.K. Warder, *Indian Buddhism*, (Delhi, India: Motilal Banarsidas, 1980), p. 10.

[13]David Kalupahana, *Causality: The Central Philosophy of Buddhism* (Honolulu: The University Press of Hawaii, 1975), p. 163.

[14]Narada Thera, *A Manual of Abhidhamma* (Rangoon, Burma: Buddha Sasana Council, 1970), p. iii.

[15]U Thittila (1987), pp. 139-140.

[16]U Thittila (1987), p. 140.

[17]Very Venerable Taungpulu Kaba-Aye Sayadaw's lecture on *Nama-Rupa* (Burmese: *nam-yoke*) given in 1978 during his first visit to U.S. at a temporary monastery on Skyline Blvd., Palo Alto, CA.

[18]Ledi Sayadaw, trans. U Nyana Maha Thera, *A Manual of Insight* (Kandy, Sri Lanka: Buddhist Publication Society, 1975), pp. 16-17.

[19]Nyanatiloka, *Guide Through the Abhidhamma Pitaka* (Columbo, Ceylon: Bauddha Sahitva Sabha, 3rd ed.), 1971, p. xiii.

[20]Narada Thera (1956), p. iii.

[21]Very Venerable Taungpulu Kaba-Aye Sayadaw, Discourse given at 56 U Wisera Road, Rangoon, Burma, 1970.

[22]Narada Thera (1956), p. v.

Chapter 2

[1]Bertrand Russell, *A History of Western Philosophy* (New York: Simon and Schuster, 1945), p. 45.

[2]Piyadassi Thera, *The Buddha's Ancient Path* (London: Rider, 1964), p. 14.

[3]Russell (1945), p. 45.

[4]Rollo May, *Man's Search for Himself* (New York: W.W. Norton, 1953), p. 14.

[5]Y. Karundasa, "The Philosophical Basis of Early Buddhist Thought," *Buddhist Quarterly*, Vol. 8, No. 9, (Summer, 1975), p. 10.

[6]S. Radhakrishnan, trans., *The Dhammapada* (London: Oxford University Press, 1966), p. 98, verse 118.

[7]Abraham Wolf, "Ethics," *Encyclopedia Britannica* (1957), VIII, p. 757.

[8]T.W. Rhys Davids and Mrs. C.A.F. Rhys Davids, trans., *Dialogues of the Buddha*, IV (London: Pali Text Society, 1973), pp. 187-188.

[9]Satischandra Chatterjee and Dhirendramohan Datta, *Introduction to Indian Philosophy* (Calcutta, India: University of Calcutta Press, 1968), p. 138.

[10]*Ibid.*, p. 138.

[11]William James, *The Philosophy of William James* (New York: The Modern Library, 1958), p. 188.

[12]John J. McDermott, ed., *The Writings of William James*, (New York: Random House, 1967), p. 784.

[13]Nolan Pliny Jacobson, *The Religion of Analysis* (George Allen & Unwin, Ltd., 1966), pp. 49-50.

[14]Christmas Humphreys, *A Popular Dictionary of Buddhism* (New York: Citadel Press, 1963), p 31.

[15]Carl Jung, *Memories, Dreams, and Reflections*, trans. Aniela Jaffe (New York: Random House, Inc., 1989), p. 274.

[16]Carl Jung, *Collected Works*, Vol. 98, il, 2nd ed. (Princeton, NJ: Princeton University Press, 1978), p. 176.

[17]Carl Jung, *Memories, Dreams and Reflections* (New York: Vintage Books, 1965), p. 177.

[18]Aldous Huxley, *The Perennial Philosophy* (New York: Harper and Row, 1970), p. 28.

[19]Roger Walsh and Frances Vaughan, eds., *Beyond Ego* (Los Angeles: Jeremy P. Tarcher, 1980), pp. 19-20.

[20]Roger Walsh and Frances Vaughan, eds., *Paths Beyond Ego* (The Putnam Publishing Group, 1993), p. 3.

[21]*Ibid.*, p. 20.

[22]*Ibid.*, p. 2

[23]Radhakrishnan (1966), p. 94, verse 103.

[24]Walsh and Vaughn (1993), p. 3

[25]Fedor Stcherbatsky, *The Conception of Buddhist Nirvana* (Leningrad: The Academy of Sciences of U.S.S.R., 1927), p. 1.

[26]Piyadassi Thera, (1964), p. 63.

[27]H. Saddhatissa, *Buddhist Ethics: Essence of Buddhism* (New York: George Brazillar, 1970), p. 30.

[28]*Ibid.*, p. 30.

[29]*Ibid.*, p. 31

[30]Radhakrishnan (1966), p. 149, verse 285.

[31]Nyanaponika Thera, *The Heart of Buddhist Meditation* (New York: Samuel Weiser, 1973), p. 72.

[32]Narada Thera, *The Dhammapada* (Taiwan: The Corporate Body of the Buddha Educational Foundation, 1993), v. 1-2, pp. 1-5.

Chapter 3

[1]A.J. Ayer, ed., *Logical Positivism* (Glencoe, IL: The Free Press, 1959), p. 4.

[2]Jayatellike, *Early Buddhist Theory of Knowledge* (London: George Allen and Unwin, 1963), p. 361.

[3]H.C. Warren, *Buddhism in Translation* (New York: Atheneum, 1970), p. 148.

[4]*Ibid.*, pp. 149-150.

[5]S. Radhakrishnan, trans., *The Dhammapada* (London: Oxford University Press, 1966), p. 146, verses 277-279.

[6]*Oxford English Dictionary* (Oxford: Oxford University Press, 1986), Vol. II.

[7]Rune E.A. Johansson, *Dynamic Aspects of Early Buddhist Psychology* (1979), p. 125

[8]B.C. Law, *Designation of Human Types*, (London: Luzac, 1969), vii.

[9]George Grimm, *The Doctrine of the Buddha* (Delhi: Motilal Banarsidass, 1982), p. 67.

[10]Johansson (1979), p. 133.

[11]George Grimm (1982), p. 67.

[12]Piyadassi Mahathera, *The Buddha's Ancient Path*, (London: Rider, 1964), p. 46.

[13]Henry Clarke Warren, *Buddhism in Translation*, (New York: Atheneum, 1970), p. 129.

[14]Nyanaponika, *The Heart of Buddhist Meditation*, (New York: Samuel Weiser, 1988), p. 35.

[15]Ledi Sayadaw, *The Manual of Buddhism* (Rangoon, Burma: Union Buddha Sasana Council, 1965), p. 109.

[16]Very Venerable Taungpulu Tawya Kaba-Aye Sayadaw, *Maha Satipatthana Vipassana-Insight Meditation* (Rangoon, Burma: Department of Religious Affairs, 1979), p. 34.

[17]*Ibid.*, p. 36

[18]Rune E.A. Johansson, *Psychology of Nirvana* (Garden City, NY: Doubleday & Co., 1970), p. 63.

[19]B.C. Law (1969), p. 55

[20]Bhikkhu Nanamoli and Bhikkhu Bodhi, trans. *The Middle Length Discourses, Majjhima Nikaya,* (Boston: Wisdom Publications, 1995), p. 715.

[21]Piyadassi Thera (1964), p. 80.

[22]Bhadantachariya Buddhaghosa, trans. Bhikkhu Nyanamoli, *The Path of Purification* (Colombo, Ceylon: M.D. Gunasena, 1964), p. 3.

[23]Radhakrishnan (1966), p. 99, verse 121.

[24]*Ibid.*, v. 122

[25]Piyadassi Thera (1964), p. 130.

[26]B.C. Law (1969), p. 20.

[27]H. Saddhatissa, *Buddhist Ethics: Essence of Buddhism* (New York: George Brazillar, 1970), p. 113.

[28]Ledi Sayadaw, *The Requisites of Enlightenment*, (Kandy: Sri Lanka, 1971), p. 125.

[29]Radhakrishnan (1966), p. 64, verses 19-20.

[30]Very Venerable Taungpulu Sayadaw's instruction. *Kinne* is a Burmese word for "getting rid of."

[31]Caroline A.F. Rhys Davids, trans., *Buddhist Manual of Psychological Ethics, Dhammasangani* (London: Pali Text Society, 1974), pp. 278-281.

[32]B. C. Law, *Designation of Human Types*, (London: Luzac, 1969), p. 23.

[33]F.L. Woodward, trans., *The Book of Gradual Sayings, Anguttara Nikaya,* Vol. II (London: Routledge & Kegan Paul Ltd., 1982), pp. 98-99.

[34]*Ibid.*

[35]*Ibid.*

[36]*Ibid.*.

[37]B.C. Law (1969), p. 20.

[38]*Ibid.*, p. 27.

[39]Very Venerable Taungpulu Tawya Kaba-Aye Sayadaw, Discourses at Taungpulu Kaba-Aye Monastery, Boulder Creek, California 1985.

[40]Epstein, Mark, *thoughts without a thinker* (New York: Basic Books, 1995), p. 211.

[41]*Dhammapada*, verses 8 and 9, translated by the author.

Chapter 4

[1]U Narada, *Conditional Relations* (London: Luzac and Company, Ltd., 1969), p. xii.

[2]McDermott, John, ed., *The Writings of William James*, "The Stream of Thought" and "The Thing and its Relations," (New York: Random House, Inc., 1968). pp. 21-74 and pp. 214-226.

[3]Narada Thera, *A Manual of Abhidhamma (Abhidhammattha-Sangaha)*, Vol. I, (Rangoon: Buddha Sasana Council, Kaba-Aye 1970), p. 5.

[4]*Ibid.*, pp. 5-6.

[5]*Dhammapada*, v. 160, translated by author.

[6]*Dhammapada*, v. 1, translated by author.

[7]*Dhammapada*, v. 71, translated by author.

[8]Ledi Sayadaw, *Manuals of Buddhism - The Expositions of the Buddha Dhamma* (Rangoon, Burma: Union Buddha Sasana Council, 1965), pp. 66-67.

Chapter 5

[1]J.B. Pratt, *The Pilgrimage of Buddhism* (New York: Macmillian, 1928), p. 6.

[2]Pratt, p. 2.

[3]Piyadassi Thera, *The Buddha's Ancient Path* (London: Rider, 1964), p. 82.

[4]Satischandra Chatterjee and Dhirendramohan Datta, *An Introduction to Indian Philosophy* (Calcutta, India: University of Calcutta Press, 1968), p. 34.

[5]Henry Clarke Warren, *Buddhism in Translation* (New York: Atheneum, 1970), p. 134.

[6]Floyd H. Ross, *The Meaning of Life in Hinduism and Buddhism* (Boston: Beacon Press, 1953), pp. 93-94.

[7]*Ibid.*, p. 95.

[8]*Ibid.*, p. 97.

[9]Kenneth K. S. Chen, *Buddhism: The Light of Asia* (Woodbury, New York: Barrons Educational Series, 1968), p. 55.

[10]Lama Anagarika Govinda, *The Psychological Attitude of Early Buddhist Philosophy* (London: Rider, 1961), p. 29.
[11]Gunapala Piyasena Malalasekera, "Some Aspects of Reality as Taught by Theravada Buddhism," *The Indian Mind*, ed. Charles A. Moore (Honolulu: East-West Center Press, 1967), p. 67.
[12]Piyadassi Thera (1964), p. 51.
[13]S. Radhakrishnan, *The Dhammapada* (London: Oxford University Press, 1966), p. 123.
[14]Pe Maung Tin, *Buddhist Devotion and Meditation* (London: S.P.C.K., 1964), p. 20.
[15]Nyanaponika Thera, trans., *Selected Buddhist Texts*, III (Kandy, Ceylon: Buddhist Publication Society, 1970), p. 4.
[16]Radhakrishnan (1966), p. 125, verse 197.
[17]Piyadassi Thera (1964), p. 18.
[18]Radhakrishnan (1966), p. 85, verse 80.
[19]Piyadassi Thera (1964), p. 82.
[20]Bhadantacariya Buddhaghosa, *The Path of Purification*, trans. Bhikkhu Nyanamoli (Colombo, Ceylon: M.D. Gunasena, 1964), p. 3.
[21]Piyadassi Thera (1964), p. 80.
[22]Radhakrishnan (1966), p. 64, verses 19-20.
[23]Piyadassi Thera (1964), p. 88.
[24]Heinrich Zimmer, *Philosophies of India*, ed. Joseph Campbell (New York; Meridian Books, 1958), p. 469.
[25]Matilal Das, *The Soul of India* (Calcutta, India: Aloka-Tirtha, 1958), pp. 93-94.
[26]Anil Kumar Sarkar, *Changing Phases of Buddhist Thought* (Patna, India: Bharati Bhawan, 1968), p. xiii.
[27]*Ibid.*, p. xii.
[28]Piyadassi Thera (1964), p. 78.
[29]Chatterjee and Datta (1968), p. 139.

Chapter 6

[1]S. Radhakrishnan, trans., *The Dhammapada* (London: Oxford Universtiy Press, 1966), p. 146.
[2]*Ibid.*, p. 145.
[3]T.W. Rhys Davids, trans. *Buddhist Suttas* (New York: Dover Publications, 1969), p. 38.

[4]Trevor Ling, *The Buddha: Buddhist Civilization in India and Ceylon* (New York: Charles Scribners Sons, 1973), p. 115.

[5]Kenneth W. Morgan, *The Path of the Buddha* (New York: Ronald Press, 1956), pp. 45-46.

[6]Y. Karundasa, "The Philosophical Basis of Early Buddhist Thought," *Buddhist Quarterly*, Vol. 8, No. 9 (Summer, 1975), p. 11.

[7]*Ibid.*, p. 11.

[8]*Ibid.*, p. 12.

[9]Laurence Waddell, *The Buddhism of Tibet* (2nd ed.; Cambridge: W. Refer, 1934), p. 121.

[10]Bhadantacariya Buddhaghosa, *The Path of Purification*, trans. Bhikkhu Nyanamoli (Colombo, Ceylon: M.D. Gunasena, 1964), p. 568.

[11]Beni Madhab Barua, "Some Aspects of Early Buddhism," *The Cultural Heritage of India*, I, eds. Suniti Kumar, Chatterji, et al. (2nd ed.; Calcutta, India: The Ramakrishna Mission Institute of Culture, 1958), p. 444.

[12]*Ibid.*, p. 444.

Chapter 7

[1]M. Hiriyanna, *Outlines of Indian Philosophy* (Bombay, India: George Allen and Unwin, 1973), p. 198.

[2]Swami Vireswarananda, *Brahma-Sutras* 4th ed. (Calcutta, India: Advaita Ashrama, 1970), p. 197, v. 25.

[3]Yamakami Sogen, *Systems of Buddhistic Thought* (Calcutta, India: Calcutta University Press, 1912), p. 102.

[4]*Ibid.*, p. 106.

[5]S. Radhakrishnan, ed., *History of Philosophy: Eastern and Western*, I (London: George Allen and Unwin, 1957), p. 178.

[6]Bhikkhu J. Kashyap, *The Abhidhamma Philosophy*, I (Patna, India: Buddha-Vihara Nolanda, 1954), pp. 36-37.

[7]Sogen (1912), p. 120.

[8]Sogen (1912), p. 155.

[9]Sogen (1912), p. 156.

[10]Kashyap (1954), I, pp. 45-47.

[11]Narada Maha Thera, *A Manual of Abhidhamma* (Kandy, Ceylon: Buddhist Publication Society, 1968), p. 78.

[12]Kashyap (1954), I, p. 51.

[13]*Ibid.*, p. 49.

[14]*Ibid.*, p. 46.
[15]Sogen (1912), p. 156.
[16]*Ibid.*, p. 157.
[17]*Ibid.*, p. 157.
[18]*Ibid.*, p. 157.
[19]*Ibid.*, p. 158.
[20]Kashyap (1954), p. 36.
[21]Very Venerable Taungpulu Kaba-Aye Sayadaw, evening discourse at 56 U Visara Road, Rangoon, Burma, 1968.
[22]Har Dayal, *The Bodhisattva Doctrine in Buddhist Sanskrit Literature* (Delhi: Motilal Banarsidass, 1970), p. 278.
[23]Sogen (1912), pp. 186-187.
[24]Frederick J. Streng, *Emptiness: A Study in Religious Meaning* (Nashville, New York: Abingdon Press, 1967), pp. 195-196.
[25]Sogen (1912), p. 14 [translated from Sanskrit by the author.]
[26]Streng (1967), p. 193, v. 12.
[27]*Ibid.*, p. 213.
[28]T.R.V. Murti, *The Central Philosophy of Buddhism: A Study of the Madhyamika System* (London: George Allen and Unwin, 1960), p. 58.
[29]Anil Kumar Sarkar, *Changing Phases of Buddhist Thought* (Patna, India: Bharati Bhawan, 1968), p. 36.
[30]Murti (1960), p. 122.
[31]Junjiro Takakusu, *The Essentials of Buddhist Philosophy*, eds. Wing-tsit Chan and Charles A. Moore (Bombay, India: Asia Pub-lishing House, 1956), p. 110.
[32]*Ibid.*, p. 83.
[33]Kenneth W. Morgan, *The Path of the Buddha: Buddhism Interpreted by Buddhists* (New York: Ronald Presss, 1956), p. 167.
[34]P.V. Bapat, ed., *2500 Years of Buddhism* (New Delhi, India: Ministry of Information and Broadcasting, Government of India, 1956), p. 108.
[35]Sogen (1912), p. 258.
[36]*Ibid.*, p. 217.
[37]*Ibid.*, p. 218.
[38]*Ibid.*, p. 218.
[39]*Ibid.*, p. 228.
[40]*Ibid.*, p. 259.
[41]*Ibid.*, pp. 213-214.

Chapter 8

[1]Mrs. C.A.F. Rhys Davids, ed., *Compendium of Philosophy* (London: Luzac, 1956), p. 10.

[2]Yamakami Sogen, *Systems of Buddhistic Thought* (Calcutta, India: Calcutta University Press, 1912), p. 172.

[3]Sogen (1912), p. 173.

[4]Anil Kumar Sarkar, *Changing Phases of Buddhist Thought* (Patna, India: Bharati Bhawan, 1968), p. 92.

[5]*Ibid.*, p. 93.

[6]*Ibid.*, p. 94.

[7]Radhakrishnan, ed., *History of Philosophy Eastern and Western*, II (London: George Allen and Unwin, 1957), p. 446.

Appendix A

[1] F.L. Woodward, trans. *The Book of the Kindred Sayings, Samyutta Nikaya*, Part III (London: Pali Text Society, 1975), p. 128.

[2]Maurice Walshe, trans. *The Long Discourses of the Buddha, Digha Nikaya*, (Boston: Wisdom Publications, 1995), p. 131

[3]S. Radhakrishnan, *The Dhammapada* (London: Oxford University Press, 1966), p. 64, verses 19-20.

[4]Frederic Spiegelberg, *Living Religions of the World* (Englewood Cliffs, N.J.: Prentice Hall, 1956), p. 246.

[5]Bhikkhu Nanamoli and Bhikkhu Bodhi, trans. *The Middle Length Discourses of the Buddha, Majjhima Nikaya*, (Boston: Wisdom Publications, 1995), p. 131.

[6]Radhakrishnan (1966), p. 94, verse 103.

[7]The Very Venerable Taungpulu Tawya Kaba-Aye Sayadaw, *Mahasatipatthana Vipassana Meditation*, trans. U Chit Tin (Rangoon, Burma: Department of Religious Affairs, 1979), p. 42.

Glossary of Pali Terms

abhi: great, highest, about, concerning
abhinibatti: rebirth
abhiññā: six higher powers, super knowledge- (1) magical powers, (2) extraordinary hearing, (3) knowledge of the thoughts of others, (4) extraordinary perception, (5) remembrance of past lives, (6) extinction of all cankers
abhisamaya: truth realization, realization of the *dhamma*, state of insight held by a noble one (*ariyapuggala*)
abhūta: unborn, uncreated, unoriginated
acatapabbaja: renunciate, one who has renounced the world to gain liberation
ācāriya: teacher
ācāriyaparamparā: lineage of teachers
ācinnaka-kamma: habitual *kamma*
acintiya: unthinkable, incomprehensible, these are: (1) the sphere of a buddha, (2) the states of meditative absorptions (*jhānas*), (3) the full implications of *kamma*, (4) metaphysical speculation concerning the origin and end of the universe
adhamma: immoral, evil, unjust deed
adhimokkha: determination, resolve, firm decision
āditta: fire
adosa: non-hate, hatelessness
adhisīla: higher virtue
aggamahāpaṅḍita: highest title for intellectual teacher of the *dhamma*
agha: pain
āhāra: food, that which sustains the corporeal
ahetuja: without roots or cause
ahiṁsā: non-violence
ahosi-kamma: ineffective *kamma*
ajāta: that which will not be born again
ājiva: livelihood
ajjava: honesty, integrity
ākāsa: space
akathaṁkathā: freedom from too much talk, doubt and speculation

akāla: timeless
akkodha: freedom from hatred
akappa cetovimutti: unshakeable deliverance of the mind
akusala: unwholesome act
ālaya: store-house, reliance, thing relied upon
alobha: greedlessness, unselfishness
amāta: deathless, final liberation from the wheel of birth and death
amoha: non-delusion, wisdom
anāgāmi: non-returner, one who has attained the second stage of sainthood towards final liberation
ānāpāna-sati: mindfulness of in-out breathing (a type of meditation)
anattā: no soul, no self
anicca: impermanence, a basic feature of all conditioned phenomena
añña: highest knowledge, gnosis, that knowledge attained by either buddha or an arahat
anupassana: contemplation
anussati: recollection, meditation, contemplation. The six recollections are (1) recollection of the buddha, (2) of his doctrine, (3) of the community of monks and nuns, (4) of morality, (5) of liberality, (6) of heavenly beings
appamāda: carefulness
appamāṇa: that which cannot be measured
appanā: sustained absorption, attainment concentration
arahat: a finally-attained one, a killer of the enemies, defilements, an enlightened being, one who has attained the final stage of liberation, holy one
ariya (also *ariya-puggala*): noble, noble person. They are of four types: (1) the stream winner (*sotāpanna*), (2) the once-returner (*sakadāgāmi*), (3) the non-returner (*anāgāmi*), (4) the noble one (*arahat*)
ariya-sacca: noble truth
arūpa: formlessness, immateriality
asaṅkhata: uncompounded
asaṅkhārika-citta: state of consciousness which has arisen spontaneously, unprompted or unhesitated moment of consciousness
asāra: essenceless
āsava: cankers, corruptions, biases, influxes
āssāda: enjoyment, attraction
asubha: loathsomeness, foulness
asuddha: impure
asura: demons, titans, ghosts, those sentient beings inhabiting those planes of existence lower than the animal plane
attā: soul, self, ego
aṭṭhaṅgika-magga: the eightfold path (to the cessation of suffering)
avacara: sphere, realm, world. The three spheres are (1) sensuous sphere (*kāmāvacara*), (2) fine-material sphere (*rūpāvacara*), (3) immaterial sphere (*arūpāvacara*)
avihiṁsā: harmlessness, non-violence, absence of cruelty

avijjā: ignorance, nescience
avirodha: non-obstruction
āyatana: (1) the twelve bases upon which the mental processes depend, corresponding to the five sense organs plus mind-base, and their corresponding objects, e.g., eye or visual organ plus visible object, also (2) sphere, another name for the four immaterial absorptions
bala: powers. The five most basic powers are (1) faith (*saddhā*), (2) energy (*vīriya*), (3) mindfulness (*sati*), (4) concentration (*samādhi*), (5) wisdom (*paññā*)
bhante: sir, venerable sir
bhava: becoming, process of existence [consisting of three planes: (1) sensuous existence (*kāma-bhava*), (2) fine-material existence (*rūpa-bhava*), (3) immaterial existence (*arūpabhava*)
bhāvanā: mental development, contemplation, meditation, culturing of the mind, mental culture
bhavaṅga-sota: subconscious life-continuum, undercurrent of life, subconscious life-stream
bhikkhu: monk
bhikkhunī: nun, member of the holy community (*saṅgha*)
bhisakka: doctor, physician
bodhi: awakening, enlightenment, supreme knowledge
bodhisatta: enlightened being, a future buddha. In Theravāda tradition, bodhisattahood is secondary to the higher ideal of arahatship. In the Mahāyāna tradition, emphasis is placed on the bodhisattva vow in which the bodhisattva, moved by compassionate zeal, vows to postpone his own entrance into *nirvāṇa* until all other sentient beings may also gain their liberation
buddha: the enlightened one, the awakened one
buddhadhamma: the teaching of all Buddhas
buddhavacana: the word of the Buddha
buddhavisaya: the domain of the Buddhas, about Buddhism
cakka: wheel, for example, *bhava-cakka*, the wheel of life or the *dhamma-cakka*, the wheel of the blessed teaching
cakkhu: eye
carita: nature, character
cetanā: volition
cetasika: mental factors, mental concomitants arising due to a given moment of consciousness (*citta*)
cetovimutti: emancipation by way of attainment of the free state of consciousness
chanda: will, desire, intention
citta: mind, consciousness, state of consciousness
citta-kkhaṇa: consciousness-moment, the time occupied by any one stage in the cognitive series (*cittavithi*) or perceptual process
citta-vithi: process of consciousness, perceptual process, cognitive series
cittekāggata: one-pointedness of mind
dāna: alms-giving, generosity, liberality

dassana: vision endowed with understanding

deva: heavenly being, deity, celestial being, a sentient being occupying the planes of existence above the human plane, a god

dhamma: doctrine, law, righteousness, order, nature, teaching, religion, quality, thing, phenomenon, constitution, norm, morality, piety, force, element, truth

dhamma cakka: wheel of the law or teaching

dhamma cakkhu: eye of truth

dhamma cariya: teacher of the *dhamma*, an official term given to a qualified teacher in Theravāda Buddhist tradition

dhātu: elements, realms. This may refer to: (1) the four physical elements: earth (*pathavidhātu*), water *(apo-dhātu)*, fire (*tejo-dhātu*), wind (*vāyo-dhātu*; or (2) the eighteen physical and mental elements upon which the process of perception depends. Also, added to the twelve bases (*āyatana*) are corresponding consciousness elements, for example, to the visual organ, eye, and the visible object, is added the eye consciousness

dīpa: island

diṭṭhi: view, belief, speculation, opinion, insight

domanassa: grief, sadness

dosa: hatred, anger, ill-will

dravya: substance

dukkha: suffering, pain, bad condition, dissatisfaction, the first noble truth [a characteristic common to all life within the bounds of *saṃsāra*]

dukkha-dukkha: intrinsic suffering

ekarasa: homogeneous

ekāsanikaṅga: the practice of eating all solid food to be taken in one sitting, before noon

gati: destiny, destination, going (to extinction)

gaṇḍa: wound

gotrabhū: one who has joined the succession of noble ones, in other words, a stream winner (*sotāpanna*)

hetu: cause, condition, root

hīnayāna: small vehicle, lesser vehicle [a term coined by mahāyānists, referring to early or orthodox Buddhism]

hiri: shyness

iddhī-pāda: the road to power

indriya: faculty [twenty-two in number, they are divided between the physical, mental, and supramundane in nature]

jarā: old age, decay

jarā-maraṇa: old age and death

jāti: birth

javana: impulsion, the active moments in the cognitive process in which *kamma* is produced

jhāna (skt: *dhyāna*): absorption, trance. It is a meditative state in which the five hindrances (*nivaraṇa*) are suppressed, allowing the arising of the factors of absorption. In the first *jhāna* of the fine-material sphere, applied thought (*vitakka*), sustained application (*vicāra*), rapture (*pīti*), joy (*sukha*), and concentration (*samādhi*) are present. As one proceeds through the higher *jhānas*, one by one these factors are eliminated until in the final absorption of the fine-material sphere, equanimity (*upekkhā*) replaces concentration and equanimity alone remains. This is the starting point for progression through the immaterial absorptions (*arūpa-jhāna*) and the attainment of the spiritual powers (*abhiññā*).

jīva: life, vital principle

jīvita (*jīvitindriya*): life, vitality, either physical or mental [the latter is one of seven universal mental factors common to all states of consciousness]

kalāpa: group, unit, the very small unit of time in which the dhammas (elements) are said to arise into existence and pass away

kāma: bodily passions, sense-pleasures

kāmacchanda: desire for sensual gratification, lust

kāmesu-micchācāra: unwholesome conduct with regard to sensual things, improper sexual conduct

kamma (skt: *karma*): action, volitional activity, either wholesome or unwholesome

kammannata: adaptability

kammanta: action

kandha: doubt

kappa (skt: *kalpa*): an aeon, world-period, an epoch of time which is inconceivably long

karuṇā: compassion, one of the four sublime abodes (*brahma-vihāra*)

kasiṇa: device, a colored pot or disc or piece of the earth used in *samatha* (calm) meditation to calm the mind, develop concentration (*samādhi*), and attain the fine-material absorptions (*rūpa-jhāna*). the ten *kasiṇas* are: (1) earth, (2) water, (3) fire, (4) wind, (5) blue, (6) yellow, (7) red, (8) white, (9) space, and (10) consciousness

kathinayāna: difficult path or career

kāya: group, body

kāyā-gata-sati: mindfulness of the body, oftentimes refers only to meditation concerning the thirty-two parts of the body

kāyānupassana: contemplation of the body, one of the four stations of mindfulness (*satipaṭṭhāna*)

khandha (skt:*skandha*): group, aggregate, heap of clinging. Five in number, the *khandhas* comprise what is normally called an "individual" or person. They are: matter aggregate (*rūpa-khandha*), feeling (*vedanā*), perception (*saññā*), mental formations (*saṅkhāra*), and consciousness (*viññāṇa*)

khanti: patience, forbearance, tolerance

khaṇika: momentariness

kilesa: defilements, unwholesome qualities

kiriya: functional, inoperative

kukkucca: worry, remorse

kusala: wholesome, profitable, moral action, good, skillful, meritorious
kusala-vipāka: the kārmic result of wholesome action
lobha-carita: greedy-natured
loka: world
lokiya: mundane
lokuttara: supramundane [concerning the path, fruition and attainment of *nibbāna*]
loṇarasa: salt
magga: path
mahā: great
mahābhūta: the four great primary elements: fire, water, earth, air
mahāggata: exalted, developed, supernormal
mahāthera: a great elder, a title indicating ten years of being a thera
mahāyāna: great vehicle Buddhism
majjhima: middle
majhima-patipada: middle path
māna: conceit, pride
mānasa desanā: initial conception, exposition in the mind
manasikara (skt: *manaskara*): attention, advertence, reflection
mano (skt: *manas*): mind
maraṇa: death, dying
mati: intellect, reason
mātika: mnemonic aid
metta: loving-kindness, amity [one of the four sublime abodes (*brahma-vihāra*)], universal love
micchā-diṭṭhi: false view, wrong opinion
middha: torpor, stupidity, sluggishness
moha: delusion, deception
mudita: sympathetic (or altruistic) joy, joy for the success or happiness of others
mūla: root
nāma: mind, mentality, name
nāma-rūpa: mind and body, name and form, mental and physical energies
nāṇa (skt: *jnāna*): knowledge, comprehension, insight, wisdom
nevāsaññānāssaññāyatana: the sphere of neither perception nor non-perception, the name for the fourth absorption of the immaterial sphere (*arūpavacara*)
nibbāna (skt: *nirvāṇa*): extinction (of greed, hate and delusion), the highest and ultimate goal of buddhist meditation, total cessation, ultimate reality
nibatti: arising, generation, rebirth, production
nikāya: sections of the *sutta piṭaka*
nimitta: cause, mark, sign, condition
niraya: hell, downward path
nirodha: cessation, extinction
nirodha-samāpatti: attainment of extinction

nissaraṇa: freedom, liberation

nivaraṇa: hindrance, obstacle, impediment. They are: (1) sense desire (*kāmacchanda*), (2) ill will (*vyāpāda*), (3) sloth and torpor (*thīna-middha*), (4) restlessness and worry (*uddhaccakukkucca*), and (5) doubt (*vicikiccā*)

niyama: natural order, lawfulness

ottappa: moral dread, shame, shyness

pabbajjā: the going forth (from the home to the homeless life)

paccaya: condition (for that which has conditionally or dependently arisen), requisite (for the monk or nun)

pacekka-buddha (skt: *pratyeka-buddha*): independently-enlightened one, one who comprehends the *dhamma* on his own effort without having heard it from a teacher

padhāna: effort. The four supreme efforts are: (1) to prevent the arising of an unwholesome state of consciousness, (2) to cut off an unwholesome state of consciousness once it has arisen, (3) to enable the arising of a wholesome state, and (4) to sustain a wholesome state of consciousness once it has arisen

pakiṇṇaka cetasika: particular mental factors

pānātipāta veramanī: abstinence from the killing of any sentient being

pañca-sīla: five moral precepts, minimum moral obligations or rules of conduct for the buddhist

pañcakkhandha: five aggregates or heaps [also called *pañcupādānakkhanda* or the five aggregates of clinging]

paññā: understanding, wisdom, knowledge, insight

paññatti-sīla: prescribed morality, as distinguished from natural morality (*pakati-sīla*)

paññāvimutti: emancipation by way of development of reason, insight or knowledge

paññindriya: reason as a guiding faculty or principle

paramattha (skt: *paramārtha*): highest, ultimate sense

pārami (skt: *pāramita*): perfection. The ten qualities which must be perfected for the attainment of the buddhahood are (1) generosity (*dāna-pārami*), (2) morality (*sīla-pārami*), (3) renunciation (*nekkhamma-pārami*), (4) wisdom (*paññā-pārami*), (5) energy (*viriya-pārami*), (6) patience (*khanti-pārami*), (7) truthfulness (*sacca-pārami*), (8) resolution (*adhiṭṭhāna-pārami*), (9) loving-kindness (*metta-pārami*), (10) equanimity (*uppekhā-pārami*)

parinibbāna: enlightenment without the physical base, that is, at death, the enlightened being 'enters' *parinibbāna*.

pariñña: full understanding or comprehension

passaddhi: relaxation, peacefulness of mind

paṭiccasamuppāda (skt: *pratityasamutpāda*): dependent origination, the doctrine of the conditionality of all mental and physical phenomena, law of conditioned origin, conditioned genesis

paṭigha: resentment, repugnance, anger

pātimokkha: disciplinary code for the ordained saṅgha. There are 227 rules of conduct for the monks and nuns

paṭipadā: road, path, way
paṭipannaka: path-attainer
paṭivedha: penetration, deep understanding
phala: fruit, results of path-attainment
phassa (skt: *sparsa*): contact, sense impression
phaya: lord, an honorific term for a spiritual teacher [Burmese]
piṭaka: basket. They refer to the baskets in which the Pāli canonical writings (on leaves) were originally placed
pīti: rapture, joy, enthusiasm, happiness
puggala (skt: *pudgala*): individual, person
pūjā: (1) homage, respect, (2) devotional service, worship ceremony
puṇṇa: moral merit, virtue
puthujjana: worldling, ordinary human being (in contrast to the path-attainer)
rāga: lust, greed, desire
rasa: essence
ratana: jewel, gem
ratana-ghara-sattāha: week of the house of gems
ritta: empty
roga: disease
rūpa: matter, material form, visible matter, visible form
sabba: all
sacca (skt: *satya*): truth
sacca-ñāṇa: knowledge of the truth
saddhā: faith, confidence, belief
sādhāraṇa: common, ordinary
sādhu: in Pāli chanting or at the end of meditation, a signature meaning "let it be", "so be it", or "excellent"
sahajayāna: easy path
sakadāgāmī: once-returner [the second stage on the path to final realization]
sākya: the name of the clan into which Siddhattha was born
sākyamuni: sage of the sākyas, a name for the buddha
salāyatana: the six sense organs including the mind
salla: an arrow
samādhi: concentration, one-pointedness of mind
samaṇa: philosopher, a novice monk
samatha: tranquillity, calmness, serenity
samathayāna: path to tranquillity
samatha-vipassana: tranquillity and insight (meditation)
saṁkhata: compounded
sammā: right
sammā-diṭṭhi: right view
sammā kammanta: right action
samma-sambodhi: perfect enlightenment
saṁsāra: round of rebirth, cycle of continuity, ocean of birth and death, cycle of becoming

samudāya-sacca: truth of the origin (of suffering), the second noble truth
saṅgha: the community of buddhist monks and nuns. [In an informal use of the word, *saṅgha* refers to the whole community of buddhists, laypersons as well as monks and nuns.]
saṅkappa: thought
saṅkhāra: mental formations, conditioned states, volitional activity
saṅkhāra-dukkha: suffering due to mental formations
saṅkarika: accompanied by
saññā: perception
santati: theory of continuum of a person and a thing
śaraṇa: refuge in the Buddha, *dhamma*, *saṅgha*
sāsana: teaching period of the buddha, the buddhist religion, teaching, doctrine
sati: mindfulness, awareness, one of the seven factors of enlightenment (*bojjhaṅga*), and one of the five spiritual faculties and powers (*bala*)
satipaṭṭhāna: foundations of mindfulness, awareness of mindfulness, setting-up of mindfulness. The four foundations of mindfulness are: (1) contemplation of body (*kāyānupassana*), (2) feelings (*vedanānupassana*), (3) mind (*cittānupassana*), (4) states (*dhammānupassana*)
satta: living being, sentient being
sāvaka: disciple, hearer, meditator
sayadaw (Burmese): senior monk, religious teacher
sikkhā: training
sīla: morality, virtue
sobhana: good, beautiful, pure, wholesome
somanassa: gladness, joyfulness
sotāpanna: stream-winner, one who has had a brief touch with the *nibbānic* state
sotāpatti: stream entry
subha-nimitta: beautiful object of attraction (to the mind)
sugati: thus gone, a happy state of existence, good state
sukha: pleasant, happiness, joy, bliss, pleasurable, case, comfort
suñña: voidness, emptiness
sutta: scripture, sermon, discourse, text
taṇhā: thirst, desire, craving
taṇhākkhaya: extinction of thirst
tapa: austerity
tathāgata: a perfect one, one who has thus-come and thus-gone, one who has found truth
tathāṭa: suchness, isness
tāvatiṁsa: a class of thirty-three devas (celestial beings) in the sensuous planes of existence (*kāmāvacara loka*)
tawya (Burmese): hermit
thera: an elder or respected teacher within the *saṅgha*
theravāda: way of the elders school of buddhism, doctrine of the elders

thīna-middha: sloth and torpor, languor and sluggishness

tilakkhaṇa: the three characteristics of existence: impermanence (*anicca*), suffering (*dukkha*), and no-self (*anattā*)

tipiṭaka: the three baskets, the three main divisions of the Pāli canon: the basket of discipline (*Vinaya piṭaka*), the basket of discourses (*Sutta piṭaka*) and the basket of the highest teaching (*Abhidhamma piṭaka*)

tiratana: triple gem or jewels: Buddha, *dhamma*, and *saṅgha*

tisaraṇa: triple refuge in the buddha, *dhamma* and *saṅgha*

tuccha: false

tusita: a plane of existence in the heavenly spheres of the sensuous worlds (*kāmāvacara loka*)

udāna: songs

uddhacca: restlessness, one of the ten fetters (*saṁyojana*) and five hindrances (*nivaraṇa*)

upācāra: moment of access

upādāna: grasping, clinging, attachment

upāsaka: a lay buddhist, layman, male

upāsika: a female layperson

upekkhā: equanimity

uposatha: the full-moon and new-moon days of the month when the monks read the *patimokkha*, the disciplinary code, in a general assembly, and laypersons observe eight precepts (*attha-sīla*)

vācā: speech

vaibhāsa: a commentary on the abhidhamma

vasavatti: a heavenly plane where deities live over 216 million years

vatthunī: rules of conduct

vedanā: feeling, sensation

vicāra: sustained thought

vicikicchā: skeptical doubt

vihāra: abode, dwelling place, monastery

vimokkha: liberation

vimutti: deliverance, emancipation

viññāṇa: consciousness, cognition

vipāka: *kamma* resultant

viparināma-dukkha: suffering as change

vipassana: insight, analytical wisdom

vipassanayāni: one who follows the path of knowledge

vipatti: aberration, deviation

virāga: detachment, absence of lust

virati: the three abstinences

viriya: energy, diligence, one of the seven factors of enlightenment (*bojjhaṅga*)

visuddhi: purification

vitakka: applied thought, thought conception, contact

vithī: process, street, cognitive series

viveka: discrimination, detachment, seclusion

vyāpāda: ill-will, anger, hatred

yāma-deva: another classification of heavenly beings in the sensuous sphere
yamaka-patihāriya: twin miracle in which lord Gotama Buddha manifested both fire and water from his body at the same time
yakka: spirit
yathābhūta-dassana: seeing things as they really are
yāna: vehicle, vessel
yogāvacara: a meditator, religious aspirant

Bibliography

Aik, Lim Teong. A *Glossary of Buddhist Terms In Four Languages: English, Chinese, Pali and Sanskrit.* Penang, Malaya: Bukit Glugar, 1960.

Avon, Henri. *Buddhism,* trans. Douglas Scott. New York: Walker, 1962.

Bahm, Archie J. *7he World's Living Religions.* New York: Dell, 1964.

Ballon, Robert, Friedrich Spiegelberg, Horace L. Friess, eds. *The Bible of the World.* New York: Viking Press, 1955.

Bancroft, Anne. *Religions of the East.* New York: St. Martin's Press, 1974.

Bapat, P.U., ed. *2500 Years of Buddhism.* New Delhi, India: Ministry of Information and Broadcasting Government of India, 1956.

Basham, A.L. *The Wonder that was India: A Survey of the Culture of the Indian Subcontinent Before the Coming of the Muslims.* New York: Grove Press, 1954.

Bateson, Gregory. *Mind and Nature.* New York: Bantam Books, 1988.

Bhagvat, Durga N. *Early Buddhist Jurisprudence.* Poona, India: Oriental Book Agency,1939.

Bhikshu, Rastrapal. *An Exposition of Karma and Rebirth.* Bengal, India: Bibhash De, 1965.

Buddhaghosa, Bhadantacariya. *The Path of Purification,* trans. Bhikku Nyanamoli. Colombo, Ceylon: M.D. Gunasena, 1964.

Burtt, E.A., ed. *The Teachings of the Compassionate Buddha.* New York: Mentor Books, 1955.

Capra, Fritjof. *The Turning Point.* Toronto: Bantam Books, 1982.

Carus, Paul. *The Gospel of Buddha.* Tucson, Arizona: Omen Press, 1972.

Chatterjee, Satischandra and Dhirendramohan Datta. *An Introduction to Indian Philosophy.* Calcutta, India: University of Calcutta Press, 1968.

Chatterji, Suniti Kumar, and others, eds. *The Cultural Heritage of India.* 4 Vols. 2nd ed. Calcutta, India: The Ramakrishna Mission Institute of Culture, 1958-62.

Chaudhuri, Haridas. *Mastering the Problems of Living.* New York: Citadel Press, 1968.

Ch'en, Kenneth K.S. *Buddhism: The Light of Asia.* Woodbury, New York: Barron's Educational Series, 1968.

Conze, Edward, trans. *Buddhist Scriptures.* Baltimore, Maryland: Penguin Books, 1959.

________ . *Buddhist Thought In India: Three Phases of Buddhist Philosophy.* Ann Arbor, Michigan: University of Michigan Press, 1970.

________, ed. *The Perfection of Wisdom in Eight Thousand Lines and Its Verse Summary.* Bolinas, Ca.: Four Seasons Foundation, 1973.

Coomaraswamy, Ananda K. *Buddha and the Gospel of Buddhism.* London and New York: Harper and Row, 1964.

Daing, U Than. *Cittānupassana and Vedanānupassana.* Rangoon, Burma: Daw San Yee, 1970.

________ . *The Doctrine of Paticcassamuppāda.* Rangoon, Burma: Rangoon Gazette, 1967.

Das, Matilal. *The Soul of India.* Calcutta, India: Aloka-Tirtha, 1958.

Dayal, Har. *The Bodhisattva Doctrine in Buddhist Sanskrit Literature.* Delhi and Patna and Varanasi, India: Modlal Banarsidass, 1932.

DeBary, Theodore, ed. *The Buddhist Tradition: In India, China, and Japan.* New York: The Modern Library, 1969.

Donath, Dorothy C. *Buddhism for the West: Theravada, Mahāyāna, Vajrayāna.* New York: Julian Press, 1971.

Dutt, Nalinaksha. *Aspects of Mahāyāna Buddhism and Its Relation to Hinayāna.* London: Luzac, 1930.

________ . *Early Monastic Buddhism.* Calcutta, India: Calcutta Oriental Book Agency, 1960.

Epstein, Mark. *Thoughts without a Thinker.* New York: Basic Books, 1995.

Fromm, Erich. *For the Love of Life.* New York: The Free Press, 1986.

Gard, Richard A., ed. *Buddhism.* New York: George Braziller, 1962.

Goddard, Dwight, ed. A *Buddhist Bible.* Boston: Beacon Press, 1970.

Goleman, Daniel. *The Meditative Mind.* Los Angeles: Jeremy P. Tarcher,1988.

________. *Emotional Intelligence.* New York: Bantam Books, 1995.

Govinda, LamaAnagatika. *ThePsychological Attitudeof Early Buddhist Philosophy.* London: Rider, 1961.

Grimm, George. *Buddhist Wisdom: The Mystery of the Self,* trans., Carroll Aikens, Delhi, Varanasi, Patna, India: Motilal Banarsidass, 1978.

Hackin, J. and others. *Asiatic Mythology.* New York: Crescent Books, [n.d.].

Hewage, L.G. *Benefits of Metta.* Colombo, Ceylon: Middle Path International, [n.d.].

Hiriyanna, M. *Outlines of Indian Philosophy.* Bombay, India: George Allen and Unwin, 1973.

Horner, I.B., trans. *The Middle Length Sayings.* 3 Vols. London: Luzac, 1967-1975 (1922-33).

________, trans., *Milinda's Questions.* 2 Vols. London: Luzac, 1969.

Humphreys, Christmas, ed. *The Wisdom of Buddhism.* New York and Evanston: Harper Colophon, 1970.

Huxley, Aldous. *The Perennial Philosophy.* New York: Harper and Row, 1970.

Jacobson, Nolan Pliny. *Buddhism: The Religion of Analysis.* Carbondale: Southern Illionois University Press, 1974.

James, William. *The Philosophy of William James.* New York: The Modern Library, 1958.

Johanson, Rune E.A. *The Dynamic Psychology of Early Buddhism.* Scandinavian Institute of Asian Studies, London and Malmo: Curzon Press, 1979.

________ . *The Psychology of Nirvana.* Garden City, N.Y.: Doubleday and Co., 1970.

Jung, Carl. *Memories, Dreams and Reflections.* trans. Anita Jaffe. New York: Random House Inc., 1989.

________ . *Collected Works.* Vol. 98, ii, 2nd ed. Princeton, N.J.: Princeton University Press, 1978.

Kashyap, Bikkhu J. *The Abhidhamma Philosophy: or the Psycho-Ethical Philosophy of Early Buddhism.* 7 Vols. Patna, India: Buddha-Vihara Nalanda, 1954.

________, ed. *The Dhammasaṅgani.* Varanasi, India: Pali Publication Board, 1960. (In Pali).

________ , ed. *The Vibhanga.* Varanasi, India: Pali Publication Board, 1960. (In Pali).

Kern, H., trans. *Saddharma-Puṇḍarika or the Lotus of the True Law.* New York: Dover Publications, 1963.

Khin, Ba. *The Real Values of True Buddhist Meditation.* Rangoon, Burma: Buddha Sāsana Council Press, 1962.

King, Winston L. *In the Hope of Nibbāna: An Essay on Theravada Buddhist Ethics.* La Salle, Ill.: Open Court, 1964.

Law, B.C. *Designation of Human Types.* London: Luzac, 1969.

Lester, Robert C. *Theravada Buddhism In Southeast Asia.* Ann Arbor, Michigan: University of Michigan Press, 1973.

Ling, Trevor. *The Buddha: Buddhist Civilization in India and Ceylon.* New York: Charles Scribner and Sons, 1973.

Maslow, Abraham. *Religions, Values, and Peak Experiences.* New York: Penguin Books, 1976.

Maung, E.U. *Taranagon and Its Merit* Rangoon, Burma: Burma Sāsana Council, 1969.

May, Rollo. *Man's Search For Himself.* New York: W.W. Norton, 1953.

McDermott, John J. *The Writings of William James.* New York: Random House, 1967.

Moore, Charles A., ed. *The Indian Mind.* Honolulu: East-West Center Press, 1967.

Morgan, Kenneth W. *The Path of the Buddha: Buddhism Interpreted by Buddhists.* New York: Ronald Press, 1956.

Morreale, Don, ed. *Buddhist America.* Santa Fe: John Muir Publications, 1988.

Muller, Max F., ed. *The Sacred Books of the East.* Vol. 35, *The Questions of King Milinda,* trans. T.W. Rhys Davids. London: Oxford University Press, 1925.

________, and others. *Studies In Buddhism.* Calcutta, India: Susil Gupta, 1953.

Murti, T.R.U. *The Central Philosophy of Buddhism: A Study of the Madhyamika System.* London: George Allen and Unwin, 1960.

Nanamoli, Bhikkhu. *The Life of the Buddha.* Kandy, Ceylon-Buddhist Publication Society, 1978.

________ . *The Guide.* London: Luzac, 1962.

Nanamoli, Thera, trans. *Mindfulness of Breathing: Ānāpānasati.* Kandy, Ceylon: Buddhist Publication Society, 1964.

________. trans. *The Practice of Lovingkindness.* Kandy, Ceylon: Buddhist Publication Society, 1964.

________. (Vol. 1) and Nyanaponika Thera (Vol. II and III), trans. *Selected Buddhist Texts.* 3 Vols. Kandy, Ceylon: Buddhist Publication Society, 1964-70.

Nanananda, Bhikkhu. *Concept and Reality in Early Buddhist Thought.* Kandy, Ceylon: Buddhist Publication Society, 1971.

Narada, Maha Thera. A *Manual of Abhidhamma.* Kandy, Ceylon: Buddhist Publication Society, 1968.

Narada, Thera, trans. *Everyman's Ethics: Four Discourses of the Buddha.* Kandy, Ceylon: Buddhist Publication Society, 1966.

_______. *Buddhism in a Nutshell.* Rangoon, Burma: Buddha Sāsana Council, 1970.

Narasu, P. Lakshmi. *What Is Buddhism?.* 3rd ed. Calcutta, India: Maha Bodhi Society of India, 1964.

Nimalasuria, Dr. A., ed. *Buddha The Healer: The Mind and Its Place in Buddhism.* Kandy, Ceylon: Buddhist Publication Society, 1971.

Nivedita, Sister. *Siva and Buddha.* Calcutta, India: Udbodhan Office [n.d.].

Nyanaponika, Thera. *Abhidhamma Studies: Researchers in Buddhist Psychology.* Kandy, Ceylon: Buddhist Publication Society, 1965.

________ . *The Heart of Buddhist Meditation.* New York: Samuel Weiser, 1988.

________ . *The Power of Mindfulness.* San Francisco: Unity Press, 1972.

________ , ed. *The Three Basic Facts of Existence.* Kandy, Ceylon: Buddhist Publication Society, 1974.

Nyanatiloka. *Buddhist Dictionary: Manual of Buddhist Terms and Doctrines.* Kandy, Sri Lanka: Buddhist Publication Society, 1980.

_______, trans. *The Word of the Buddha.* Colombo, Ceylon: The Word of the Buddha Publishing Committee, 1952.

_______. *Path To Deliverance.* Kandy, Sri Lanka: Buddhist Publication Society, 1982.

Nyanatiloka, Maha Thera. *Guide Through the Abhidhamma Piṭaka.* Kandy, Ceylon: Buddhist Publication Society, 1971.

Oldenberg, Dr. Hermann. *Buddha: His Life, His Doctrines, His Order,* trans. William Haey. Varanasi and Delhi, India: Indological Book House, 1971.

Ornstein, Robert E. *The Nature of Human Consciousness: A Book of Readings*. San Francisco: W.H. Freeman, 1973.

Pe, Maung Tin. *Buddhist Devotion and Meditation*. London: S.P.C. K., 1964.

_______ . *The Exposition: Buddhaghosa's Commentary on the Dhammsaṅgani or The First Book of the Abhidhamma Piṭaka*. 2 Vols. London: Luzac, 1958.

_______ . *The Path of Purity*, being a translation of Buddhaghosa's *Visuddhimagga*. London, Eng.: Pali-Text Society, 1975. (Translation series no. 11, 17, 21).

Piyadassi, Thera. *The Buddha's Ancient Path*. London: Rider, 1964.

Prabhavananda, Swami. *The Spiritual Heritage of India*. 2nd ed. Hollywood: Vedanta Press, 1969.

Pratt, J.B. *The Pilgrimage of Buddhism*. New York: Macmillian, 1928.

Radhakrishnan, ed. *History of Philosophy Eastern and Western*. 2 Vols. London: George Allen and Unwin, 1957.

_______, trans. *Dhammapada*. London: Oxford University Press, 1966.

Rahula, Walpola. *What the Buddha Taught*. New York: Grove Press, 1959.

Ramanan, K.U. *Nagarjuna's Philosophy as Presented in the Mahāprajñā-Pāramitā Śāstra*. Rutland, Vermont: Charles E. Tuttle, 1966.

Rhys Davids, C.A.F.. *The Birth of Indian Psychology and Its Development in Buddhism*. London: Luzac, 1936.

_______, ed. A *Buddhist Manual of Psychological Ethics*. London and Boston: Pali Text Society, 1974.

_______ , ed. *Compendium of Philosophy*. London: Luzac, 1956 .

_______. *Gotama The Man*. London: Luzac, 1928.

_______. *Psalms of the Early Buddhists*. London: Pali-Text Society, 1980.

________. *Sakya: or Buddhist Origins.* London: Kegan Paul, Trench, Trubner, 1931.

Rhys Davids, T.W., trans. *Buddhist Suttas.* New York- Dover Publications, 1969.

________, trans. *The Questions of King Milinda.* New York: Dover Publications, 1963.

________ and Mrs. C.A.F. Rhys Davids, trans. *Dialogue of the Buddha.* 4 Vols. London: Pali-Text Society, 1973.

________ and Paul Debes, eds. *Tevijja Sutta: A Discourse oj' the Buddha on the Path to God.* Kandy, Ceylon: Buddhist Publication Society.

Ross, Floyd H. *The Meaning of Life in Hinduism and Buddhism.* Boston: Beacon Press, 1953.

Russell, Bertrand. A *History of Western Philosophy.* New York: Simon and Schuster, 1945.

Saddhatissa, H. *Buddhist Ethics: Essence of Buddhism.* New York: George Braziller, 1970.

Sarkar, Anil Kumar. *Changing Phases of Buddhist Thought.* Patna, India: Bharati Bhawan, 1968.

Sayadaw, Maha-Thera Ledi, Aggamahapandita. *The Manuals of Buddhism.- The Expositions of the Buddha-Dhamma.* Rangoon and Kaba-Aye, Burma: Union Buddha Sāsana Council, 1965.

________ . *The Manual of Insight. Vipassana Dīpānī,* trans. Nyana Maha-Thera. Kandy, Ceylon: Buddhist Publication Society, 1961.

Sayadaw, Venerable Mahasi. *Buddhist Meditation and Its Forty Subjects. Rangoon,* Burma: Buddha Sāsana Council Press, 1957.

________. *Practical Insight Meditation.* San Francisco: Unity Press, 1972.

________ . *The Satipaṭṭhāna Vipassana Meditation.* San Francisco: Unity Press, 1971.

Sharma, Chandradhar. A *Critical Survey of Indian Philosophy.* 2nd ed. Delhi and Varanasi and Patna, India: Motilal Banarsidass, 1964.

Sogen, Yamakami. *Systems of Buddhistic Thought*. Calcutta, India: Calcutta University Press, 1912.

Sole-Leris, Amadeo. *Tranquility and Insight, an introduction to the oldest forms of Buddhist Meditation*. Boston: Shambhala, 1986.

Soma, Thera. *The Removal of Distracting Thoughts*. Kandy, Ceylon: Buddhist Publication Society, 1972.

Spiegelberg, Frederic. *Living Religions of the World*. Englewood Cliffs, N.J.: Prentice Hall, 1956.

Stcherbatsky, Fedor. *The Conception of Buddhist Nirvana*. Leningrad: The Academy of Sciences of the U.S.S.R., 1927.

Streng, Frederick J. *Emptiness: A Study in Religious Meaning*. Nashville, New York Abingdon Press, 1967.

Stryk, Lucien, ed. *World of the Buddha: A Reader*. Garden City, New York: Anchor Books, 1969.

Takakusa, Junjiro. *The Essentials of Buddhist Philosophy*, eds. Wing-tsit Chan and Charles A. Moore. Bombay and Calcutta and New Delhi, India: Asia Publishing House, 1956.

Tart, Charles T., ed. *Transpersonal Psychologies*. New York and London: Harper and Row, 1975.

Taungpulu Tawya Monastery,ed. *The Methodical Practice of Mindfulness*. Burma: Taungpulu Tawya Monastery, 1969.

Thittila, Pathamakyan Ashin, trans. *The Book of Analyses: 7he Second Book of the Abhidhamma Piṭaka*. London: Luzac, 1969.

________ . *Essential Themes of Buddhist Lectures*. Bangkok, Thailand: Mabamaku-RajaVidyalaya Press, 2529 B.C.

U Chit Tu. trans. *Five Nikāyas*. Rangoon, Burma: English Editorial Board, Department of Religious Affairs, 1977.

Vajiranana, Parawahera and Francis Story. *The Buddhist Doctrine of Nibbana*. Kandy, Ceylon: Buddhist Publication Society, 1971.

Van Gorkom, Nina. *Abhidharma in Daily Life*. Bangkok, Thailand: Dhamma Study Group, 1975.

Vipassana Reseach Association. *What Buddhism Is*. Rangoon, Burma: Buddhist-Sāsana Council Press, 1951.

Vireswarananda, Swami. *Brahma Sutras.* 4th ed. Calcutta, India: Advaita Ashrama, 1970.

Waddell, Lawrence. The Buddhism of Tibet. 2nd ed. Cambridge: W. Heffer, 1934.

Walsh, Roger and Frances Vanghan, eds. *Beyond Ego.* Los Angeles: Jeremy P. Tarcher, 1980.

________. *Paths Bevond Ego.* The Putnam Publishing Group, 1993.

Warder, A. K. *Indian Buddhism.* Delhi, India: Motilal Banarsidass, 1980.

Warren, Henry Clarke. *Buddhism In Translations.* New York: Atheneum, 1970.

Welbon, Guy Richard. *7he Buddhist Nirvana and Its Western Interpreters.* Chicago and London: University of Chicago Press, 1968.

Wolf, Abraham. "*Ethics,* " Encyclopedia Britannica, 1957, VIII, 757-761.

Zimmer, Heinrich. *Philosophies of India,* ed. Joseph Campbell. New York: Meridian Books, 1958.

NON-BOOK MATERIAL

Abeyasekera, Richard. "The Master's Quest For Light," *Bodhi Leaves,* No.7 (1962).

Engler, Jack. "You Have To Be Somebody Before You Can Be Nobody," *Inquiring Mind,* 5 (Summer).

Karundasa, Y. "The Philosophical Basis of Early Buddhist Thought," *Buddhist Quarterly,* Vol. 8, No. 9 (Summer, 1975), 10-17.

Malalusekera, Dr. G.P. "Buddhism and Worship," *Bodhi Leaves,* No. A.8 (1964).

Naroda, Thera. "An Outline of Buddhism," *Bodhi Leaves,* No. A.I. (1968).

Naravira, Thera. "Mindfulness and Awareness," *Bodhi Leaves,* No. B.60 (1973).

Nyanponika Thera. "The *Abhidhamma*: Buddhist Philosophy," *The Light of Buddha* (August, 1960), pp. 6-12.

Phaya, Most Venerable Taungpulu Sayadaw. Address for Tingyan Festival. Rangoon, Burma, April 14, 1969.

Quittner, Irene. "Hate-As Unwholesome Root," *Bodhi Leaves,* No. A.16 (1971).

Sayadaw, Venerable Thazi. Address for Burmese New Year's Day. Rangoon, Burma, April 16, 1969.

Story, Francis. "Buddhist Lay Ethics," *Bodhi Leaves,* No. 59 (1972).

________. "Two Essays: *Saṃsāra* and The Way of Dispassion," *Bodhi Leaves,* No. B.49 (1970).

Teik, Boon. "*Moha Citta* or Deluded Mind in Buddhist Psychology," *The Light of Buddha* (January, 1964), pp. 9-17.

About the Author

Rina Shyamcharan Sircar was born in Rangoon, Burma. She received her M.A. and law degrees from Rangoon University, and she earned doctorate degrees from the University of Gujarat, India and the California Institute of Asian Studies.

In 1974, at the invitation of Dr. Haridas Chaudhuri, she began teaching in San Francisco at the California Institute of Asian Studies (now Integral Studies) which Dr. Chaudhuri founded. From 1988-1992 she held the Haridas Chaudhuri Chair of Comparative and South Asian Studies. Since 1995 she has held the World Peace Buddhist Studies Chair. Rina's specialized fields are Abhidhamma Pitaka, Sutta Pitaka, and Pali language.

Rina was trained in the Theravāda forest tradition. In 1981, she co-founded the Taungpulu Kaba-Aye Monastery in Boulder Creek, California with her teacher, the late Very Venerable Taungpulu Tawya Kaba-Aye Sayadaw of Burma. In 1985 she co-founded the Taungpulu Kaba-Aye Meditation Center in San Francisco. She has given *satipatthana-vipassana* retreats around the world since 1974. She does healing and also gives classes and workshops on healing and death and dying.